The Due Process of Law

'For I think it an undeniable position,
that a competent knowledge of the laws
of that society, in which we live, is
the proper accomplishment of every
gentleman and scholar; an highly useful,
I had almost said essential, part of liberal
and polite education'.

Sir William Blackstone at the opening of
the Vinerian lectures, 25 October 1758.
(*Commentaries* I.5).

The
Due Process
of Law

by the Rt Hon
LORD DENNING
Master of the Rolls

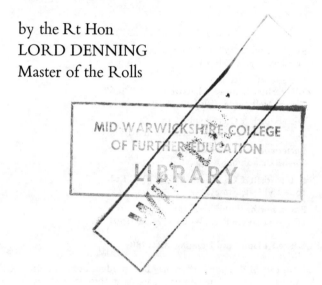
London
BUTTERWORTHS
1980

England	Butterworth & Co (Publishers) Ltd
London	88 Kingsway, WC2B 6AB
Australia	Butterworths Pty Ltd
Sydney	586 Pacific Highway, Chatswood, NSW 2067
	Also at Melbourne, Brisbane, Adelaide and Perth
Canada	Butterworth & Co (Canada) Ltd
Toronto	2265 Midland Avenue, Scarborough M1P 4S1
New Zealand	Butterworths of New Zealand Ltd
Wellington	77—85 Customhouse Quay
South Africa	Butterworth & Co (South Africa) (Pty) Ltd
Durban	152—154 Gale Street
USA	Butterworths (Publishers) Inc
Boston	10 Tower Office Park, Woburn, Mass 01801

ISBN Casebound 0 406 17607 8
        Limp 0 406 17608 6

Typeset by Scribe Design, Gillingham, Kent
Printed in Great Britain by Billing & Sons Limited
Guildford, London and Worcester

Preface

Last year I wrote *The Discipline of Law*. This year I decided
to try another. On somewhat different lines. Not so much on
the subjects taught in the Law Schools of Universities. But
more on the practical working of the law. I venture to call it
The Due Process of Law. By 'due process' I do not mean
rules of procedure. They are far too dull. I mean much
the same as Parliament meant when it first used the phrase.
It was in 1354 in the Statute of 28 Edw. III, ch. 3:

'That no man of what estate or condition that he be, shall
be put out of land or tenement, nor taken nor imprisoned,
nor disinherited, nor put to death, without being brought
in answer by due process of the law'.

I mean also much the same as Madison meant when he
proposed an amendment to the Constitution of the United
States. It was accepted in 1791 in the fifth amendment:
'No person . . . shall be deprived of life, liberty, or property,
without due process of law'.

So by 'due process of law' I mean the measures authorised
by the law so as to keep the streams of justice pure: to see
that trials and inquiries are fairly conducted; that arrests and
searches are properly made; that lawful remedies are readily
available; and that unnecessary delays are eliminated. It is in
these matters that the common law has shown its undoubted
genius. I have attempted to show the problems that have
confronted us in these fields since the war: and the way in
which they have been solved or attempted to be solved. With
what success I must leave you to judge. Many proposals have
been made by us in the Court of Appeal. Time and again we
have ventured out on a new line: only to be rebuffed by the

House of Lords. On the ground that the legislature – advised by this body or that – can see all round; whereas the Judges see only one side. This I dispute. The Judges have better sight and longer sight than those other bodies: especially in the practical working of the law and in the safe-guarding of individual freedom. And when it is said that some other body should first investigate and report, I ask: 'How long, O Lord (Chancellor), how long?'

In the choice of topics, I have tried to do – what the cobbler should do – to stick to his last – to those topics of which I have most experience. I have chosen them also for their general interest. Not bookish law which depends on the interpretation of Statutes or Rules of Court. But the law in which persons count. So I tell you about the cylinder of laughing gas; and the judge who talked too much; and the ship which sank without trace; and the wife who was deserted. Behind each of these stories there is a lesson of practical importance. That is why I have told them.

Remember, too, that much of our substantive law is found laced in with procedures. So I would wish this book to be a companion volume to *The Discipline of Law*. If there are among you some who will become solicitors, I hope that I may sign – or my successor may sign – for you the certificate which the Master of the Rolls signs for everyone who is admitted a solicitor:

'Whereas, upon Examination and Enquiry touching your fitness and capacity to act as a Solicitor of the Supreme Court, I am satisfied that you are a fit and proper person so to act, I do by this writing under my hand ADMIT you to be a Solicitor of the Supreme Court'.

More rarely, perhaps, if there are some of you who are 'utter' barristers – that is to say, if you are 'outer' barristers, practising outside the Bar in the Law Courts – I may say – or my successor may say – when you come to the Court of the Master of the Rolls:

'Her Majesty, having been pleased to appoint you one of her Counsel learned in the law, will you be pleased to take your seat without the bar accordingly'.

In any case, whatever your *role*, I would as Master of the *Roles*, remind you that it is, in the long run, on the maintenance of law and order that civilised society depends. So, if it would please you, read this book as well as the other.

Denning.

November, 1979

Contents

Part seven
THE DESERTED WIFE'S EQUITY

Part eight
THE WIFE'S SHARE IN THE HOME

Table of Cases

Part one

Keeping the streams of justice clear and pure

Introduction

Since I became Master of the Rolls in 1962 there have been many important developments in the law of Contempt of Court. I have been concerned in most of them. Previously there had been no recourse to the Court of Appeal. All the decisions were by courts of first instance. It was only in 1960 that an appeal was first given. So it has been the function of the Court of Appeal to enunciate the principles — save for one case which went to the House of Lords, the *Thalidomide case*. Even in that case the decision of the Lords met with a rebuff from the European Court of Human Rights. The Court of Appeal was restored. The cases are worth the attention of the lawyers — for the sake of the principles — but are even more worth the interest of the laymen — for the sake of the stories they tell. So I have told the tale.

I have divided the account into chapters. Each considers a different facet of the single diamond. It was Lord Hardwicke who said in 1742:

'There cannot be anything of greater consequence than to keep the streams of justice clear and pure, that parties may proceed with safety both to themselves and their characters'[1].

There is not one stream of justice. There are many streams. Whatever obstructs their courses or muddies the waters of any of those streams is punishable under the single cognomen 'Contempt of Court'. It has its peculiar features. It is a criminal offence but it is not tried on indictment with a

1. *The St. James' Evening Post case* (1742) 2 Atkins 469 at 472.

3

jury. It is tried summarily by a judge alone, who may be the very judge who has been injured by the contempt. These features have led to some concern. Commentators have criticised it. Committees have considered it. A Discussion Paper has been presented to Parliament. So I have tried to collect our cases upon it. Its importance is undoubted. Of all my learned friends, Francis Mann is the most learned of all. Long ago, as a young man, he came from Germany. Since then he has become the head of an important firm of City solicitors: and at the same time the exponent in our literature of a wealth of legal knowledge. In the July 1979 issue of *The Law Quarterly Review* (page 348) he writes:

'Contempt of Court is undoubtedly one of the great contributions the common law has made to the civilised behaviour of a large part of the world beyond the continent of Europe where the institution is unknown'.

It is that great contribution to which I now turn.

1 In the face of the Court

1 In my own presence

It is an old phrase — 'contempt in the face of the Court'. It means a contempt which the Judge sees with his own eyes: so that he needs no evidence of witnesses. He can deal with it himself at once.

The most quoted case goes back to the year 1631. It was at Salisbury on the Western Circuit. A prisoner threw a brickbat at the Judge of Assize. It was originally reported in Norman-French. That was the language which was commonly in use by lawyers and reporters at that time. But put into English, the translation is given in 3 Dyer at 188b:

'Richardson Chief Justice of C.B. at the assizes at Salisbury in the summer of 1631 was assaulted by a prisoner condemned there for felony, who after his condemnation threw a brickbat at the said Judge which narrowly missed; and for this an indictment was immediately drawn by Noy against the prisoner, and his right hand cut off and fixed to the gibbet, upon which he was immediately hanged in the presence of the Court'.

I have often told of that case to the students with the apocryphal addition:

'The Judge had his head on one side on his hand as the brickbat whizzed past. Straightening himself up, he said, "If I'd been an upright judge, I should no longer be a judge" '.

Leaving reported cases I can give evidence of what I have seen with my own eyes. I was a junior waiting in the Court of Appeal for my case to be reached. It was in the Court next to Carey Street. Just before the midday adjournment, a man got up from the row behind me. He threw a tomato at the Judges. It was not a good shot. It passed between Lords Justices Clauson and Goddard. It hit the panelling with a loud squish. They were taken aback. They adjourned for a few minutes. Then they returned, had him brought up, and sentenced him straightaway to six weeks' imprisonment.

Later on, when I was sitting as a Lord Justice in the same Court with Lord Justice Bucknill, it was similar but not the same. It was a hot day. Counsel were talking a lot of hot air. A man got up with his stick and smashed the glass window. To let in some fresh air, I suppose. At any rate we did not commit him for contempt of court. We sent him off to Bow Street to be dealt with for malicious damage.

Still later, when I was presiding, we became more lenient. On every Monday morning we hear litigants in person. Miss Stone was often there. She made an application before us. We refused it. She was sitting in the front row with a book-case within her reach. She picked up one of Butterworth's 'Workmen's Compensation Cases' and threw it at us. It passed between Lord Justice Diplock and me. She picked up another. That went wide too. She said, 'I am running out of ammunition'. We took little notice. She had hoped we would commit her for contempt of court — just to draw more attention to herself. As we took no notice, she went towards the door. She left saying: 'I congratulate your Lordships on your coolness under fire'.

2 The Welsh students invade the Court

It was a dramatic case. Students of Wales were very enthusiastic about the Welsh language and they were very upset because the programmes to Wales were being broadcast in English and not in Welsh. They demonstrated to make a protest. They came up to London. They invaded the Court. I could see their point of view: for I have a special relationship with Wales. During the First World War I was a second lieutenant in the Royal Engineers. I myself am, of course, English on both sides, from time without memory. But I was posted to the 151st Field Coy. of the Royal Engineers which was attached to the 38th (Welsh) Division. I wore on my arm-flash the Red Dragon of Wales. I served with them in France. One of my proudest records (I was just 19) is an entry in the history of the Welsh Division recording the night of 23/24 August 1918 when we advanced across the river Ancre under heavy shell and rifle fire:

'Meanwhile two battalions of the 115th Brigade had crossed the Ancre at Aveley over a bridge made by the 151st Field Company RE under the supervision of Lieutenants Denning and Butler and formed up on a one battalion frontage on the left of 113th Brigade'.

A simple entry of a brave occasion. But I record it now because of some comments I received after the case of the Welsh students, *Morris v Crown Office*[1].

It was the first case in which the Court of Appeal had to consider 'contempt in the face of the Court'. Eleven young students had been sentenced to prison. Each for three months. They were all from the University of Aberystwyth. They were imbued with Welsh fervour. They had been sentenced on Wednesday, 4 February 1970. I always see that urgent cases are dealt with expeditiously. We started their appeal on Monday, 9 February and decided it on Wednesday, 11 February. I also have some say in the constitution of the Court. So I arranged for one of the Welsh Lords Justices to sit. Lord Justice Arthian Davies was well qualified. He was not only Welsh. He could speak Welsh. He sat with Lord Justice Salmon and me. We heard the argument on the Monday and Tuesday. We discussed the case on Wednesday morning and delivered judgment on the Wednesday afternoon. We had to do it so quickly that I hope you will excuse its imperfections. But these are some extracts from it[2]:

1. [1970] 2 QB 114.
2. Ibid. at 121 and 125.

7

'Last Wednesday, just a week ago, Lawton J, a judge of the High Court here in London, was sitting to hear a case. It was a libel case between a naval officer and some publishers. He was trying it with a jury. It was no doubt an important case, but for the purposes of today it could have been the least important. It matters not. For what happened was serious indeed. A group of students, young men and young women, invaded the court. It was clearly prearranged. They had come all the way from their University of Aberystwyth. They strode into the well of the court. They flocked into the public gallery. They shouted slogans. They scattered pamphlets. They sang songs. They broke up the hearing. The judge had to adjourn. They were removed. Order was restored.

'When the judge returned to the court, three of them were brought before him. He sentenced each of them to three months' imprisonment for contempt of court. The others were kept in custody until the rising of the court. Nineteen were then brought before him. The judge asked each of them whether he or she was prepared to apologise. Eight of them did so. The judge imposed a fine of £50 on each of them and required them to enter into recognisances to keep the peace. Eleven of them did not apologise. They did it, they said, as a matter of principle and so did not feel able to apologise. The judge sentenced each of them to imprisonment for three months for contempt of court.

'In sentencing these young people in this way the judge was exercising a jurisdiction which goes back for centuries. It was well described over 200 years ago by Wilmot J in an opinion which he prepared but never delivered. "It is a necessary incident", he said, "to every court of justice to fine and imprison for a contempt of the court acted in the face of it". That is *R v Almon* (1765) Wilm 243, 254. The phrase "contempt in the face of the court" has a quaint old-fashioned ring about it; but the importance of it is this: of all the places where law and order must be maintained, it is here in these courts. The course of justice must not be deflected or interfered with. Those who strike at it strike at the very foundations of our society. To maintain law

8

and order, the judges have, and must have, power at once to deal with those who offend against it. It is a great power – a power instantly to imprison a person without trial – but it is a necessary power. So necessary, indeed, that until recently the judges exercised it without any appeal. There were previously no safeguards against a judge exercising his jurisdiction wrongly or unwisely. This was remedied in the year 1960. An appeal now lies to this court; and, in a suitable case, from this court to the House of Lords. With these safeguards this jurisdiction can and should be maintained.

'Eleven of these young people have exercised this right to appeal: and we have put all other cases aside to hear it. For we are here concerned with their liberty: and our law puts the liberty of the subject before all else.

'At this point I would pay a tribute to the way in which Mr. Watkin Powell conducted this appeal on their behalf. He did as well as any advocate I ever heard. We have been much assisted too by the Attorney-General, who came here, not as prosecutor, but as a friend of the court. He put all the relevant considerations before us to our grateful benefit.

. . . .

'I hold, therefore, that a judge of the High Court still has power at common law to commit instantly to prison for criminal contempt, and this power is not affected in the least by the provisions of the Act of 1967. The powers at common law remain intact. It is a power to fine or imprison, to give an immediate sentence or to postpone it, to commit to prison pending his consideration of the sentence, to bind over to be of good behaviour and keep the peace, and to bind over to come for judgment if called upon. These powers enable the judge to give what is, in effect, a suspended sentence. I have often heard a judge say at common law, for ordinary offences, before these modern statutes were passed:
"I will bind you over to come up for judgment if called upon to do so. Mark you, if you do get into trouble again, you will then be sentenced for this offence. I will make a note that it deserves six months' imprisonment. So that is what you may get if you do not accept this chance".

9

'That is the common law way of giving a suspended sentence. It can be done also for contempt of court.

'I come now to Mr. Watkin Powell's third point. He says that the sentences were excessive. I do not think they were excessive, at the time they were given and in the circumstances then existing. Here was a deliberate interference with the course of justice in a case which was no concern of theirs. It was necessary for the judge to show — and to show to all students everywhere — that this kind of thing cannot be tolerated. Let students demonstrate, if they please, for the causes in which they believe. Let them make their protests as they will. But they must do it by lawful means and not by unlawful. If they strike at the course of justice in this land — and I speak both for England and Wales — they strike at the roots of society itself, and they bring down that which protects them. It is only by the maintenance of law and order that they are privileged to be students and to study and live in peace. So let them support the law and not strike it down.

'But now what is to be done? The law has been vindicated by the sentences which the judge passed on Wednesday of last week. He has shown that law and order must be maintained, and will be maintained. But on this appeal, things are changed. These students here no longer defy the law. They have appealed to this court and shown respect for it. They have already served a week in prison. I do not think it necessary to keep them inside it any longer. These young people are no ordinary criminals. There is no violence, dishonesty or vice in them. On the contrary, there was much that we should applaud. They wish to do all they can to preserve the Welsh language. Well may they be proud of it. It is the language of the bards — of the poets and the singers — more melodious by far than our rough English tongue. On high authority, it should be equal in Wales with English. They have done wrong — very wrong — in going to the extreme they did. But, that having been shown, I think we can, and should, show mercy on them. We should permit them to go back to their studies, to their parents and continue the good course which they have so wrongly disturbed.

'There must be security for the future. They must be of good behaviour. They must keep the peace. I would add, finally, that there is power in this court, in case of need, to recall them. If it should become necessary, this court would not hesitate to call them back and commit them to prison for the rest of the sentence which Lawton J passed on them.

'Subject to what my brethren will say in a few moments, I would propose that they be released from prison today, but that they be bound over to be of good behaviour, to keep the peace and to come up for judgment if called upon within the next 12 months'.

Now I return to the commentators. The reaction from England was expressed in two anonymous postcards that I received. One said 'You lousy coward'. The other said 'You ought to resign'. But the reaction from Wales was one of entire satisfaction. The newspapers applauded us. A Dean of Divinity wrote simply, 'Thank you for doing justice by our young people'.

3 The Official Solicitor comes in with the Devil

That contempt was done 'in the face of the Court'. The Judge saw it with his very eyes. He witnessed it. So he needed no evidence to prove it. Is this kind of contempt limited to what the Judge himself sees? Suppose he sees nothing himself, but he has to have witnesses to prove it. Can the Judge then try it summarily? Is the offender entitled to legal representation? Is he entitled to claim trial by jury? Those important questions came up for decision in another case. It is *Balogh v St. Albans Crown Court*[1]. Mr. Balogh was a young man of whom the newspapers took some notice: for he was the son of the distinguished economist Lord Balogh. He played a practical joke and found himself sentenced to prison. Melford Stevenson J sentenced him to six months' imprisonment. As Mr. Balogh wished to appeal he wrote to the Official Solicitor.

Now the Official Solicitor is a most useful person. He

1. [1975] 1 QB 73.

11

looks after the interests of those who cannot, or will not, look after themselves. Such as infants and persons in need of care and protection. He takes a special interest in persons committed for contempt of court: because people are sometimes a bit obstinate. Quite often a wife gets an order against her husband for the sale of the house — he disobeys it and is committed for contempt. He would rather stay in prison indefinitely than give up the house to his wife. In such a case the Official Solicitor takes up the case for him and gets him released, as in *Danchevsky v Danchevsky*[1]. Such persons often refuse to do anything to purge their contempts. They take no steps to appeal. They sit sullenly aggrieved in their prison cells. They may sit there indefinitely unless somebody does something to bring their case before the Court. So the Official Solicitor does it.

The Official Solicitor took up the case of Mr. Balogh. He lodged notice of appeal. But who was to be respondent to the appeal? It could not be the Judge. No judge can be sued, served or summoned for anything he does as a judge. So we invited the Attorney-General to appoint a counsel as *amicus curiae* — that is, as a friend of the Court — to help us. That is the practice. The Attorney-General appointed the Treasury 'Devil', Mr. Gordon Slynn. A 'devil', in the eyes of the law, is an unpaid hack. When I started at the Bar, I often looked up cases and even wrote opinions for a barrister senior to me — and was not paid a penny. I 'devilled' for him. I did it to get experience. It is different now. A 'devil' is always paid for his work. The Treasury 'Devil' is the best of devils. He is the pick of the juniors at the Bar with a reversion to a judgeship. Mr. Gordon Slynn was outstanding. The best I have ever known. He will go far.

4 The 'laughing gas' does not escape

Mr. Balogh's practical joke is so entertaining — and the Judge's

1. [1975] Fam 17.

handling of it so instructive — that I would simply quote from it and let my judgment speak for itself[1]:

'There is a new Court House at St. Albans. It is air-conditioned. In May of this year the Crown Court was sitting there. A case was being tried about pornographic films and books. Stephen Balogh was there each day. He was a casual hand employed by solicitors for the defence, just as a clerk at £5 a day, knowing no law. The case dragged on and on. He got exceedingly bored. He made a plan to liven it up. He knew something about a gas called nitrous oxide (N_2O). It gives an exhilarating effect when inhaled. It is called "laughing gas". He had learned all about it at Oxford. During the trial he took a half cylinder of it from the hospital car park. He carried it about with him in his brief case. His plan was to put the cylinder at the inlet to the ventilating system and to release the gas into the court. It would emerge from the outlets which were just in front of counsel's row. So the gas, he thought, would enliven their speeches. It would be diverting for the others. A relief from the tedium of pornoggraphy. So one night when it was dark he got on to the roof of the court house. He did it by going up from the public gallery. He found the ventilating ducts and decided where to put the cylinder. Next morning, soon after the court sat, at 11.15, he took his brief case, with the cylinder in it, into court no. 1. That was not the pornography court. It was the next door court. It was the only court which had a door leading up to the roof. He put the brief case on a seat at the back of the public gallery. Then he left for a little while. He was waiting for a moment when he could slip up to the roof without anyone seeing him. But the moment never came. He had been seen on the night before. The officers of the court had watched him go up to the roof. So in the morning they kept an eye on him. They saw him put down his brief case. When he left for a moment, they took it up. They were careful. There might be a bomb in it. They opened it. They took out the cylinder. They examined it and found out what

1. [1975] 1 QB 73 at 81, 84, 85 and 86.

it was. They got hold of Balogh. They cautioned him. He told them frankly just what he had done. They charged him with stealing a bottle of nitrous oxide. He admitted it. They kept him in custody and reported the matter to Melford Stevenson J who was presiding in court no. 1 (not the pornogaphy court). At the end of the day's hearing, at 4.15 p.m., the judge had Balogh brought before him. The police inspector gave evidence. Balogh admitted it was all true. He meant it as a joke. A practical joke. But the judge thought differently. He was not amused. To him it was no laughing matter. It was a very serious contempt of court. Balogh said:
"I am actually in the wrong court at the moment. . . . The proceedings which I intended to subvert are next door. Therefore, it is not contempt against your court for which I should be tried".

The judge replied:
"You were obviously intending at least to disturb the proceedings going on in courts in this building, of which this is one. . . . You will remain in custody tonight and I will consider what penalty I impose on you . . . in the morning".

'Next morning Balogh was brought again before the judge. The inspector gave evidence of his background. Balogh was asked if he had anything to say. He said:
"I do not feel competent to conduct it myself. I am not represented in court. I have committed no contempt. I was arrested for the theft of the bottle. No further charges have been preferred".

The judge gave sentence:
"It is difficult to imagine a more serious contempt of court and the consequences might have been very grave if you had carried out your express intention. I am not going to overlook this and you will go to prison for six months. . . . I am not dealing with any charge for theft. . . . I am exercising the jurisdiction to deal with the contempt of court which has been vested in this court for hundreds of years. That is the basis on which you will now go to prison for six months".

Balogh made an uncouth insult: "You are a humourless automaton. Why don't you self-destruct?" He was taken away to serve his sentence.

'Eleven days later he wrote from prison to the Official Solicitor. In it he acknowledged that his behaviour had been contemptible, and that he was now thoroughly humbled. He asked to be allowed to apologise in the hope that his contempt would be purged. The Official Solicitor arranged at once for counsel to be instructed, with the result that the appeal has come to this court.

. . . .

'But I find nothing to tell us what is meant by "committed in the face of the court". It has never been defined. Its meaning is, I think, to be ascertained from the practice of the judges over the centuries. It was never confined to conduct which a judge saw with his own eyes. It covered all contempts for which a judge of his own motion could punish a man on the spot. So "contempt in the face of the court" is the same thing as "contempt which the court can punish of its own motion". It really means "contempt in the cognisance of the court".

'Gathering together the experience of the past, then, whatever expression is used, a judge of one of the superior courts or a judge of Assize could always punish summarily of his own motion for contempt of court whenever there was a gross interference with the course of justice in a case that was being tried, or about to be tried, or just over – no matter whether the judge saw it with his own eyes or it was reported to him by the officers of the court, or by others – whenever it was urgent and imperative to act at once. This power has been inherited by the judges of the High Court and in turn by the judges of the Crown Court.

. . . .

'This power of summary punishment is a great power, but it is a necessary power. It is given so as to maintain the dignity and authority of the court and to ensure a fair trial. It is to be exercised by the judge of his own motion only when it is urgent and imperative to act immediately – so as to maintain the authority of the court – to prevent disorder – to enable witnesses to be free from fear – and jurors from being improperly influenced – and the like. It is, of course, to be exercised with scrupulous care, and only when the case

15

is clear and beyond reasonable doubt: see *R v Gray* [1900] 2 QB 36, 41 by Lord Russell of Killowen CJ. But properly exercised it is a power of the utmost value and importance which should not be curtailed.

'Over 100 years ago Erle CJ said that ". . . these powers, . . . as far as my experience goes, have always been exercised for the advancement of justice and the good of the public": see *Ex parte Fernandez* (1861) 10 CBNS 3, 38. I would say the same today. From time to time anxieties have been expressed lest these powers might be abused. But these have been set at rest by section 13 of the Administration of Justice Act 1960, which gives a right of appeal to a higher court.

'As I have said, a judge should act of his own motion only when it is urgent and imperative to act immediately. In all other cases he should not take it upon himself to move. He should leave it to the Attorney-General or to the party aggrieved to make a motion in accordance with the rules in R.S.C., Ord. 52. The reason is so that he should not appear to be both prosecutor and judge: for that is a role which does not become him well.

'Returning to the present case, it seems to me that up to a point, the judge was absolutely right to act of his own motion. The intention of Mr. Balogh was to disrupt the proceedings in a trial then taking place. His conduct was reported to the senior judge then in the court building. It was very proper for him to take immediate action, and to have Mr. Balogh brought before him. But once he was there, it was not a case for summary punishment. There was not sufficient urgency to warrant it. Nor was it imperative. He was already in custody on a charge of stealing. The judge would have done well to have remanded him in custody and invited counsel to represent him. If he had done so counsel would, I expect, have taken the point to which I now turn.

. . . .

'When this case was opened, it occurred to each one of us: Was Mr. Balogh guilty of the offence of contempt of court? He was undoubtedly guilty of stealing the cylinder of gas, but was he guilty of contempt of court? No proceedings were disturbed. No trial was upset. Nothing untoward took place. No gas was released. A lot more had to be done by Mr. Balogh. He had to get his brief case. He had to go up to the roof. He had to place the cylinder in position. He had to open the valve. Even if he had done all this, it is very doubtful whether it would have had any effect at all. The gas would have been so diluted by air that it would not have been noticeable. . . . So here Mr. Balogh had the criminal intent to disrupt the court, but that is not enough. He was guilty of stealing the cylinder, but no more.

'On this short ground we think the judge was in error. We have already allowed the appeal on this ground. But, even if there had not been this ground, I should have thought that the sentence of six months was excessive. Balogh spent 14 days in prison: and he has now apologised. That is enough to purge his contempt, if contempt it was.

'Conclusion

'There is a lesson to be learned from the recent cases on this subject. It is particularly appropriate at the present time. The new Crown Courts are in being. The judges of them have not yet acquired the prestige of the Red Judge when he went on Assize. His robes and bearing made everyone alike stand in awe of him. Rarely did he need to exercise his great power of summary punishment. Yet there is just as much need for the Crown Court to maintain its dignity and authority. The judges of it should not hesitate to exercise the authority they inherit from the past. Insults are best treated with disdain — save when they are gross and scandalous. Refusal to answer with admonishment — save where it is vital to know the answer. But disruption of the court or threats to witnesses or to jurors should be visited with immediate arrest. Then a remand in custody and, if it can be arranged, representation by counsel. If it comes to a sentence, let it be such as the offence deserves — with the comforting reflection that, if it is in error, there is an appeal to this court. We always hear these appeals within a day or two. The present case is a good instance. The judge acted with a firmness which became him. As it happened, he went too far. That is no reproach to him. It only shows the wisdom of having an appeal'.

2 The victimisation of witnesses

1 The trade union member is deprived of his office

Now I turn to a closely related topic. Every Court has to depend on witnesses. It is vital to the administration of justice that they should give their evidence freely and without fear. Yet everyone knows that witnesses may be suborned to commit perjury – they may be threatened with dire consequences if they tell the truth – they may be punished afterwards for telling the truth. You might think it obvious that it was a gross contempt of court for anyone to intimidate or victimise a witness. Yet it was not until 1962 that this was fully debated and considered. It was in *Attorney-General v Butterworth*[1]. Mr. Butterworth and others were on the committee of the branch of a trade union. One of the members had given evidence which they disliked. He had given it before the Restrictive Practices Court. Mr. Butterworth and others determined to punish him for it. They deprived him of his office as branch delegate and treasurer. It was reported to the Attorney-General: because he has a public duty to prosecute for contempt of court. He considered that the action of Mr. Butterworth and the others was a contempt. He applied to the Restrictive Practices Court. They held it was not a contempt. The Attorney-General appealed to our Court.

Now I remember this case for a particular reason. It was argued for three days on Wednesday, Thursday and Friday, 11, 12 and 13 July 1962. It was the 'night of the long knives'.

1. [1963] 1 QB 696.

19

The Prime Minister, Mr. Harold Macmillan, dispensed with most of his ministers, at a minute's notice; they included the Lord Chancellor, Lord Kilmuir. That left him very sore. Now one of the duties of the Master of the Rolls is that he has to swear in any new Lord Chancellor. One day I was warned that I would have to swear in a new Lord Chancellor. I was not told who he was. But during that morning the Attorney-General, Sir Reginald Manningham-Buller (who was arguing the case himself), asked to be excused for an hour or two. We guessed the reason. He was to be the new Lord Chancellor. So on one day he was arguing before us as Attorney-General. The next day he was Lord Chancellor above us. We decided in his favour — but on the merit of his argument — not because he had become Lord Chancellor. Things like that make no impact on us. As in all these cases we do not delay. We prepared our judgments over the weekend and gave them on the Monday morning. He was sworn in before us on the Tuesday. In the judgment we sought to enunciate the relevant principles[1]:

'In the case of Butterworth, Bailey and Etherton, the pre-dominant motive in the minds of each of those gentlemen was to punish Greenlees for having given evidence in the R.E.N.A. case. . . .

. . . .

'I cannot agree with the decision of the Restrictive Practices Court. It may be that there is no authority to be found in the books, but if this be so, all I can say is that the sooner we make one the better. For there can be no greater contempt than to intimidate a witness before he gives his evidence or to victimise him afterwards for having given it. How can we expect a witness to give his evidence freely and frankly, as he ought to do, if he is liable, as soon as the case is over, to be punished for it by those who dislike the evidence he has given? Let us accept that he has honestly given his evidence. Is he to be liable to be dismissed from his employment, or to be expelled from his trade union, or to be deprived of his

1. [1963] 1 QB 696 at 717.

office, or to be sent to Coventry, simply because of that evidence which he has given? I decline to believe that the law of England permits him to be so treated. If this sort of thing could be done in a single case with impunity, the news of it would soon get round. Witnesses in other cases would be unwilling to come forward to give evidence, or, if they did come forward, they would hesitate to speak the truth, for fear of the consequences. To those who say that there is no authority on the point, I would say that the authority of Lord Langdale MR in *Littler v Thomson*[1] is good enough for me:

"If witnesses are in this way deterred from coming forward in aid of legal proceedings, it will be impossible that justice can be administered. It would be better that the doors of the courts of justice were at once closed".

I have no hesitation in declaring that the victimisation of a witness is a contempt of court, whether done whilst the proceedings are still pending or after they have finished. Such a contempt can be punished by the court itself before which he has given evidence, and, so that those who think of doing such things may be warned where they stand, I would add that if the witness has been damnified by it he may well have redress in a civil court for damages.

'Whilst I agree that there is no authority directly on the point, I beg leave to say that there are many pointers to be found in the books in favour of the view which I have expressed. . . .

. . . .

'In most of the cases which I have mentioned the witness had finished his evidence but the case itself was not concluded at the time when the step was taken against him. Nevertheless the principle was laid down, as I have shown, in terms wide enough to cover cases where the proceedings were concluded. And I must say that I can see no sense in limiting this species of contempt to punishment inflicted on a witness while the case is still going on. Victimisation is as great an

1. (1839) 2 Beav 129 at 131.

interference with justice when it is done after a witness gets home as before he gets there. No such distinction is drawn in the case of interference with a juror. Nor should it be drawn in the case of a witness. In *R v Martin*[1] the jury convicted one John Martin; the foreman of the jury had scarcely reached home and gone upstairs when the prisoner's brother, James Martin, called and challenged the foreman to mortal combat for having bullied the jury. This was held by the court in Ireland to be a contempt of court, as indeed it surely was. It does not matter whether the challenge was before or after he got home. Nor could it matter in the case of a judge. Nor in the case of a witness.

. . . .

'But when the act is done with mixed motives, as indeed the acts here were done, what is the position? If it is done with the predominant motive of punishing a witness, there can be no doubt that it is a contempt of court. But even though it is not the predominant motive, yet nevertheless if it is an actuating motive influencing the step taken, it is, in my judgment, a contempt of court. I do not think the court is able to, or should, enter into a nice assessment of the weight of the various motives which, mixed together, result in the victimisation of a witness. If one of the purposes actuating the step is the purpose of punishment, then it is a contempt of court in everyone so actuated.

. . . .

'We take into account the apology which has been offered by the members of the union who have been brought here, and, as it is a case of considerable importance which the Attorney-General has thought right to bring to this court, we do not think it necessary to impose the whole burden of costs on these gentlemen. . . .

'. . . . In the result, therefore, three will pay £200 apiece and the other three will pay £100 apiece, making £900 in all payable by them towards the Attorney-General's costs'.

---

1. (1848) 5 Cox CC 356.

2 The tenant is evicted from his home

Now there is an important point which arises when a witness is victimised — and suffers loss on account of it. The contemnor can be punished by the Courts by fine or imprisonment. But can the sufferer sue the contemnor for damages? I should have thought he could, or at least, should be able to do so. The victimisation is not only a criminal offence. It is, to my mind, a civil wrong — a tort as lawyers call it. This point was much discussed a few months later: and I regret to say that I found myself in a minority. It was to my mind a shocking case. A house was let out by a landlord in tenement flats. The landlord forcibly evicted one tenant called Harrand. That tenant sued the landlord for damages for wrongful eviction. Chapman, the next-floor tenant, had seen what had happened. Then these were the facts reported in *Chapman v Honig*[1]:

'. . . . Chapman had been tenant since 1959. He had seen something of what happened on the second floor, and Harrand wanted him to' give evidence in his action against the landlord described above. Chapman, fearing what might befall him if he gave evidence against his landlord, did not go voluntarily to the court. He was subpoenaed to do so, and only gave evidence in obedience to the subpoena. He gave evidence on 22 June 1962, at the hearing before Judge Baxter. On the very next day, 23 June 1962, the landlord served on Chapman notice to quit his first-floor flat on 28 July 1962. The reason he did that was simply because Chapman had given evidence for Harrand. The object of the landlord was, the judge found, "to punish or victimise Mr. Chapman for having given evidence".

. . . .

'. . . . The judge gave judgment for the plaintiff for £50 damages for contempt of court.

. . . .

'. . . . On the judge's findings the landlord gave this notice to quit and attempted to evict the tenant vindictively

1. [1963] 2 QB 502 at 504.

in order to punish Chapman for having given evidence against him. That is in itself a contempt of court — a criminal offence — and punishable accordingly (see *Attorney-General v Butterworth*[1]); and, being done by father and son in a combination to injure, it may also have been a conspiracy: see *Crofter Hand Woven Harris Tweed Co Ltd v Veitch*[2]. It was in any case unlawful. My brother Pearson LJ has, however, some doubt about it. He thinks that the victimisation of a witness is not a contempt of court *in itself*. It is only a contempt if *other* people are likely to get to know of it and be deterred from giving evidence in *other* actions. If that is right, it would mean this, that if the tenant proclaims his grievance upon the housetops, telling everyone about it, the landlord is guilty of contempt. But if the tenant should keep his suffering to himself, without telling his neighbours why he is evicted, the landlord does no wrong. That cannot be right. . . .

. . . .

'The principle upon which this case falls to be decided is simply this. No system of law can justly compel a witness to give evidence and then, on finding him victimised for doing it, refuse to give him redress. It is the duty of the court to protect the witness by every means at its command. Else the whole process of the law will be set at naught. If a landlord *intimidates* a tenant by threatening him with notice to quit, the court must be able to protect the tenant by granting an *injunction* to restrain the landlord from carrying out his threat. If the landlord *victimises* a tenant by actually giving him notice to quit, the court must be able to protect the tenant by holding the notice to quit to be *invalid*. Nothing else will serve to vindicate the authority of the law. Nothing else will enable a witness to give his evidence freely as he ought to do. Nothing else will empower the judge to say to him: "Do not fear. The arm of the law is strong enough to protect you".

1. [1963] 1 QB 696, [1963] LR 3 RP 327, [1962] 3 All ER 326, [1962] 3 WLR 819, CA.
2. [1942] AC 435, [1942] 1 All ER 142, 58 TLR 125, HL.

'It is said, however, that to hold the notice invalid is a pointless exercise, because the landlord can give another notice next day or next week or next month: and that notice will be valid. I do not agree. If the landlord has been guilty of such a gross contempt as to victimise a tenant, I should have thought that any court would hold that a subsequent notice to quit was invalid unless he could show that it was free from the taint. The landlord can at least be required to purge his contempt before being allowed to enforce the contractual rights which he has so greatly abused. The tenant, of course, has to pay his rent and perform his covenants: so there is no injustice in requiring the landlord to clear his conscience.

'The case was put of the valet who gives evidence against his master in a divorce suit. Next day the master, out of spite, dismisses him by a month's notice. Clearly the notice is unlawful. But the servant cannot stay on against the master's will. The law never enforces specifically a contract for personal service. But what are the damages? They would, I think, be such damages as a jury might assess to recompense him for the loss of the *chance* of being kept on longer, if he had not been victimised. Thus only can the law give adequate redress, as it should, to an innocent person who has been damnified for obeying its commands. . . .

. . . .

'The truth is, however, that this is a new case. None like it has ever come before the courts so far as I know. But that is no reason for us to do nothing. We have the choice before us. Either to redress a grievous wrong, or to leave it unremedied. Either to protect the victim of oppression, or to let him suffer under it. Either to uphold the authority of the law, or to watch it being flouted. Faced with this choice I have no doubt what the answer should be. We cannot stand idly by. The law which compels a witness to give evidence is in duty bound to protect him from being punished for doing it. That was the view of Judge Sir Alun Pugh when he granted an injunction. It was the view of Judge Baxter when he gave damages of £50. It is my view too. I would not turn the tenant away without remedy. I would dismiss this appeal'.

That was not the view of my two colleagues. They held that the notice to quit was valid: and that the tenant had no remedy in damages. They overruled Judge Sir Alun Pugh and Judge Baxter who I know are very good and experienced judges. They also overruled me though that does not matter so much. They even suggested that as a general proposition there can never be a right of action for damages for contempt of court. Pearson LJ said significantly (at page 522):

'The general proposition (that there can never be a right of action) might well be correct, but in the present case it is enough to say that there can be no such right of action in respect of an act which, as between the plaintiff and the defendant, has been done in exercise of a right under a contract or other instrument and in accordance with its provisions .... The same act as between the same parties cannot reasonably be supposed to be both lawful and unlawful — in the sphere of contract, valid and effective to achieve its object, and in the sphere of tort, wrongful and imposing a tortious liability'.

That decision went no further. My two colleagues went so far as to refuse the tenant leave to appeal to the Lords. No doubt because only £50 was involved. The tenant was legally aided and the landlord was not: and it would be hard on the landlord to have him taken to the Lords over such a small sum. The case is a disturbing reflection on our doctrine of precedent as recently proclaimed by the Lords. The majority decision in *Chapman v Honig* is binding on all Courts for the future unless someone comes along with the time and money — and I may add the courage — to take it to the Lords. I would venture to ask my lawyer readers: Would you advise your client to take it to the Lords?

3 Refusing to answer questions

1 Two journalists are sent to prison

Next there came a case of intense public interest. Two journalists refused to answer questions asked of them in the witness-box. They were sent to prison. Were they guilty of contempt of court?

Newspapers had been saying there was a spy in the Admiralty. Parliament ordered an inquiry. Lord Radcliffe presided over it. One of the journalists had written that 'it was the sponsorship of two high ranking officials which led to Vassall avoiding the strictest part of the Admiralty's security vetting'. Lord Radcliffe asked the journalist: 'What was the source of your information? Where did you get it from?' The journalist said: 'I decline to answer'. Lord Radcliffe asked: 'Will you inquire from the source whether he is willing for it to be divulged?' The journalist still declined to answer.

Lord Radcliffe informed the Attorney-General. He moved the Court to punish the journalist for contempt of court. Mr. Justice Gorman sentenced him to six months. The journalist appealed to our Court. It raised the question whether a journalist has any privilege in the matter.

A preliminary point arose as to the relevancy of the question. A witness is only bound to answer a relevant question, not an irrelevant one. The cases, heard together, were *Attorney-General v Mulholland; Attorney-General v Foster*[1]. I dealt with the point in this way:

1. [1963] 2 QB 477 at 487.

'Was the question relevant to the inquiry? Was it one that the journalist ought to answer? It seems to me that if the inquiry was to be as thorough as the circumstances demanded, it was incumbent on Mulholland to disclose to the tribunal the source of his information. The newspapers had made these allegations. If they made them with a due sense of responsibility (as befits a press which enjoys such freedom as ours) then they must have based them on a trustworthy source. Heaven forbid that they should invent them! And if they did get them from a trustworthy source, then the tribunal must be told of it. How otherwise can the tribunal discover whether the allegations are well founded or not? The tribunal cannot tell unless they see for themselves this trustworthy source, this witness who is the foundation of it all. The tribunal must, therefore, be entitled to ask what was the source from which the information came'.

Next I dealt with the question of privilege[1]:

'But then it is said (and this is the second point) that however relevant these questions were and however proper to be answered for the purpose of the inquiry, a journalist has a privilege by law entitling him to refuse to give his sources of information. The journalist puts forward as his justification the pursuit of truth. It is in the public interest, he says, that he should obtain information in confidence and publish it to the world at large, for by so doing he brings to the public notice that which they should know. He can expose wrongdoing and neglect of duty which would otherwise go unremedied. He cannot get this information, he says, unless he keeps the source of it secret. The mouths of his informants will be closed to him if it is known that their identity will be disclosed. So he claims to be entitled to publish all his information without ever being under any obligation, even when directed by the court or a judge, to disclose whence he got it. It seems to me that the journalists put the matter much too high. The only profession that I know which is given a privilege from disclosing information to a court of

1. Ibid. at 489.

law is the legal profession, and then it is not the privilege of the lawyer but of his client. Take the clergyman, the banker or the medical man. None of these is entitled to refuse to answer when directed to by a judge. Let me not be mistaken. The judge will respect the confidences which each member of these honourable professions receives in the course of it, and will not direct him to answer unless not only it is relevant but also it is a proper and, indeed, necessary question in the course of justice to be put and answered. A judge is the person entrusted, on behalf of the community, to weigh these conflicting interests — to weigh on the one hand the respect due to confidence in the profession and on the other hand the ultimate interest of the community in justice being done or, in the case of a tribunal such as this, in a proper investigation being made into these serious allegations. If the judge determines that the journalist must answer, then no privilege will avail him to refuse.

. . . .

'It seems to me, therefore, that the authorities are all one way. There is no privilege known to the law by which a journalist can refuse to answer a question which is relevant to the inquiry and is one which, in the opinion of the judge, it is proper for him to be asked. I think it plain that in this particular case it is in the public interest for the tribunal to inquire as to the sources of information. How is anyone to know that this story was not a pure invention, if the journalist will not tell the tribunal its source? Even if it was not invention, how is anyone to know it was not the gossip of some idler seeking to impress? It may be mere rumour unless the journalist shows he got it from a trustworthy source. And if he has got it from a trustworthy source (as I take it on his statement he has, which I fully accept), then however much he may desire to keep it secret, he must remember that he has been directed by the tribunal to disclose it as a matter of public duty, and that is justification enough.

. . . .

'. . . . We have anxiously considered the sentences of six months and three months respectively which Gorman J

29

passed on Mulholland and Foster, and after full consideration we have felt unable to adopt the view that the sentences are disproportionate to the serious nature of the offence'.

2 The *New Statesman* is angry

That case made some journalists very angry. The *New Statesman* published an article by one of them against us Judges in which he suggested that the press would retaliate:

'Any judge who gets involved in a scandal during the next year or so, must expect the full treatment'.

To which the *Daily Mirror* retorted with a nice piece of satire:

'Is it likely that Lord Denning will be copped in a call-girl's boudoir, or Lord Justice Danckwerts be caught napping flogging stolen cigarettes, or Lord Justice Donovan be caught pinching a Goya from the National Gallery? Is Mr. Justice Gorman, who sentenced the two silent journalists, likely to be discovered running a Soho strip-tease club when the Courts are in recess?

The possibility is laughably remote.

The *Mirror* recognises that it is the duty of a judge to administer the law as the law stands, and not as some would like it to be'.

Thanks be to the *Daily Mirror*!

4 Scandalising the Court

1 Lord Mansfield is criticised

When the Judges of a Court are criticised or defamed – or as
it is put 'scandalised' – they can punish the offender. They
do it, they say, not to protect themselves as individuals but
to preserve the authority of the Court. It was so stated in
one of the most eloquent passages in our law books – in a
judgment which was prepared but never delivered. The Judge
who was criticised was one of our greatest. It was Lord
Mansfield himself in 1765. He had made an amendment to
an information against John Wilkes. Now Mr. Almon had a
shop in Piccadilly. He published a pamphlet entitled 'A Letter
concerning Libels, Warrants, Seizure of Papers, &c.'. He sold
it in his shop for 1s 6d. In it he said that Lord Mansfield had
made the amendment 'officiously, arbitrarily, and illegally'.
Nowadays we are used to criticisms of that kind but in those
days the Attorney-General moved to commit Mr. Almon for
contempt of court. The case was argued and Mr. Justice
Wilmot prepared a judgment of 28 pages in length ready to
punish Mr. Almon. But Mr. Almon apologised. The Attorney-
General resigned. The proceedings were dropped. So Mr.
Justice Wilmot's judgment was never delivered. Forty years
later it was published in a volume of Wilmot's cases under
the title *R v Almon*[1]. In it he said (at page 259):

'If their authority (i.e. of the Judges) is to be trampled upon
by pamphleteers and news-writers, and the people are to be
told that the power, given to the Judges for their protection,

1. (1765) Wilm 243–271.

31

is prostituted to their destruction, the Court may retain its power some little time, but I am sure it will instantly lose all its authority; and the power of the Court will not long survive the authority of it: is it possible to stab that authority more fatally than by charging the Court, and more particularly the Chief Justice, with having introduced a rule to subvert the constitutional liberty of the people? A greater scandal could not be published'.

2 Mr Justice Avory comes under fire

We have travelled far since that time. In the 1920's the offence of 'scandalising the Court' was regarded as virtually obsolete. But it was revived in a case in 1928 when I was four years called to the Bar. I was in chambers at No. 4 Brick Court. I had few briefs. I spent much of my time editing — or helping edit — a new edition of *Smith's Leading Cases*. But I did find time to go across the Strand to listen to this *cause célèbre*. The *New Statesman* had published an article criticising Mr. Justice Avory. Now he was a Judge held by the profession with respect, almost with awe. He was a small man but resolute and stern. It showed in his face with his firm mouth and piercing grey eyes. He had tried a libel action with a jury. They had awarded £200 damages against Dr. Marie Stopes, the advocate of birth control — then much frowned upon — see *Sutherland v Stopes*[1]. The *New Statesman* denounced the case and added these words:

'The serious point in this case, however, is that an individual owing to such views as those of Dr. Stopes cannot apparently hope for a fair hearing in a Court presided over by Mr. Justice Avory — and there are so many Avorys'.

Proceedings were taken against the editor of the *New Statesman* for contempt of court. They are reported in *R v New Statesman*[2]. On the one side was the Attorney-General,

1. [1925] AC 47.
2. (1928) 44 TLR 301.

Sir Douglas Hogg KC. On the other, Mr. William Jowitt KC. Each was a brilliant advocate. Each was afterwards Lord Chancellor. But how different. Jowitt — tall, handsome and distinguished with a resonant voice and clear diction. Hogg looked like Mr. Pickwick and spoke like Demosthenes. Jowitt put it well for the *New Statesman*. He quoted a judgment by a strong Board of the Privy Council in 1899 saying:

'Committals for contempt of Court by scandalising the Court itself have become obsolete in this country. Courts are contented to leave to public opinion attacks or comments derogatory or scandalous to them' (*McLeod v St. Aubyn*[1]).

Hogg replied by quoting a passage from Wilmot's undelivered judgment upholding the offence on the ground that 'to be impartial, and to be universally thought so, are both absolutely necessary'.

Jowitt saw that the Court were against him. So he handled them tactfully. Whilst he submitted there was no contempt, he excused the article by reason of the haste in which it was written: and apologised humbly if it were held to be a contempt. That pleased the Court. They did not send the editor to prison. They adjudged that he was guilty of contempt: but they did not fine him. They only ordered him to pay the costs.

3 We ourselves are told to be silent

Oddly enough, the last case on this subject concerned Sir Douglas Hogg's son, Mr. Quintin Hogg, as he then was. In his full title, the Rt. Hon. Quintin Hogg QC, MP. Now Lord Hailsham of St. Marylebone, the Lord Chancellor, he is the most gifted man of our time. Statesman, Orator, Philosopher — he has no compare. Whilst out of office, he is by turns author, journalist, and television personality. In his exuberance he wrote for *Punch* and in 1968 found himself

1. [1899] AC 549 at 561.

brought up by Mr. Raymond Blackburn on the charge that
he was guilty of contempt of court. He criticised the Court
of Appeal in words which were quite as strong as those in
which Mr. Almon criticised Lord Mansfield. His words are
set out fully in the report of the case, *R v Commissioner
of Police of the Metropolis*[1]. He said:

'The legislation of 1960 and thereafter has been rendered
virtually unworkable by the unrealistic, contradictory and, in
the leading case, erroneous, decisions of the courts, including
the Court of Appeal . . . . it is to be hoped that the courts
will remember the golden rule for judges in the matter of
obiter dicta. Silence is always an option'.

The case came before us on a Monday morning, 26
February 1968. Mr. Blackburn applied in person. Mr. Hogg
was in Court but was represented by the most graceful
advocate of our time, Sir Peter Rawlinson QC, now Lord
Rawlinson. He told us that Mr. Hogg in no way intended to
scandalise the Court or the Lords Justices — whom he held
in the highest personal and professional regard — but he
maintained that the article constituted a criticism which he
had a right to state publicly. We accepted the submission. We
delivered judgment straightaway, as we usually do. We did not
write twenty eight pages as Mr. Justice Wilmot did. This is
what I said (at page 154):

'This is the first case, so far as I know, where this court has
been called on to consider an allegation of contempt against
itself. It is a jurisdiction which undoubtedly belongs to us
but which we will most sparingly exercise: more particularly
as we ourselves have an interest in the matter.

'Let me say at once that we will never use this jurisdiction
as a means to uphold our own dignity. That must rest on
surer foundations. Nor will we use it to suppress those who
speak against us. We do not fear criticism, nor do we resent
it. For there is something far more important at stake. It is
no less than freedom of speech itself.

1. [1968] 2 QB 150 at 154.

'It is the right of every man, in Parliament or out of it, in the press or over the broadcast, to make fair comment, even outspoken comment, on matters of public interest. Those who comment can deal faithfully with all that is done in a court of justice. They can say that we are mistaken, and our decisions erroneous, whether they are subject to appeal or not. All we would ask is that those who criticise us will remember that, from the nature of our office, we cannot reply to their criticisms. We cannot enter into public controversy. Still less into political controversy. We must rely on our conduct itself to be its own vindication.

'Exposed as we are to the winds of criticism, nothing which is said by this person or that, nothing which is written by this pen or that, will deter us from doing what the occasion requires, provided that it is pertinent to the matter in hand. Silence is not an option when things are ill done.

So it comes to this: Mr. Quintin Hogg has criticised the court, but in so doing he is exercising his undoubted right. The article contains an error, no doubt, but errors do not make it a contempt of court. We must uphold his right to the uttermost.

'I hold this not to be a contempt of court, and would dismiss the application'.

5 Disobedience to an order of the Court

1 Strict proof

One of the most important powers of a court of law is its power to give orders. Very often it has to make an order commanding a person to do something – or restraining him in some way. If he disobeys, the Court has one weapon in its armoury which it can use. It can punish him for contempt of court. Either by fine or by imprisonment. This kind of contempt has the characteristics which are common to all contempts of court. It is a criminal offence. It must be proved beyond reasonable doubt. We laid that down in *Re Bramblevale Ltd*[1]. But in addition the Court insists on several requirements being strictly observed.

2 The three dockers

This strictness was very much in evidence in the case of the three dockers, *Churchman v Shop Stewards*[2]. It arose out of the Industrial Relations Act 1971 which set up a new court, the Industrial Relations Court. It was bitterly opposed by the trade unions and their members. So much so that they refused to recognise the new court: or to obey the orders issued by it. A crisis arose when the dockers in the East End of London picketed a depot. The Court issued an order commanding them to stop the picketing. The dockers did not appear before the Court nor were they represented. They

1. [1970] 1 Ch 128.
2. [1972] 1 WLR 1094.

continued the picketing. The Industrial Relations Court gave judgment on Wednesday, 14 June 1972 (which is quoted at page 1097):

'The conduct of these men, as it appears at present, has gone far beyond anything which could appropriately be disposed of by the imposition of a fine. Unless we receive some explanation we have no alternative but to make orders committing them to prison. But we wish to give them every opportunity to explain their conduct, if it can be explained'.

The Court then set a dead-line for an explanation to be given:

'If they have not appeared before us tomorrow morning or applied to the Court of Appeal before 2 p.m. on Friday, 16 June, the warrants will issue'.

Now everyone knew that the dockers would take no notice of the Court. They would continue to disobey. They would continue their picketing. They would not appear before the Industrial Court to give an explanation. They would not apply to the Court of Appeal. The warrants would issue. They would go to prison. They would be martyrs. The trade union movement would call a general strike which would paralyse the country.

It was averted. But how was it done? The Official Solicitor appeared from nowhere. He applied to us in the Court of Appeal asking us to quash the order of the Industrial Court. We did so. The dockers were very disappointed. They were at the gates of the depot expecting to be arrested. Instead there were no warrants, no arrests, no prison, no martyrdom, no strike.

Everyone asked at once: Who is the Official Solicitor? Who put him up to this? What right had he to represent the men when they wished for no representation and what right had he to come to the Court and ask for the committal order to be quashed? On what ground was it quashed? I gave the reasons in my judgment on the fateful Friday (at page 1097):

37

'The Industrial Court gave them until 2 p.m. today, Friday, in which to apply to the Court of Appeal. The three dockers have not applied themselves, nor have they instructed anyone to apply on their behalf. But the Official Solicitor has done so. He has authority to apply on behalf of any person in the land who is committed to prison and does not move the court on his own behalf. Likewise, on behalf of any person against whom an order for committal is made, he is authorised to come to this court and draw the matter to its attention. He has instructed Mr. Pain, and Mr. Pain has submitted to us that the evidence before the Industrial Court was not sufficient to warrant the orders of committal'.

I pause here to say that Mr. Pain was very conversant with trade union matters. He was a very effective advocate. He used to assume a disarming air of diffidence as if to say, 'Please help me'. And of course we did.

I went on:

'. . . . In exercising those powers, and particularly those which concern the liberty of the subject, I would hold, and this court would hold, that any breach giving rise to punishment must be proved in the Industrial Court with the same strictness as would be required in the High Court here in this building. So we have to see whether the orders were properly proved, and the breaches of them proved, according to that degree of strictness.

. . . .

'It seems to me that the evidence before the Industrial Court was quite insufficient to prove — with all the strictness that is necessary in such a proceeding as this, when you are going to deprive people of their liberty — a breach of the court's order.

'. . . . It may be that in some circumstances the court may be entitled, on sufficient information being brought before it, to act on its own initiative in sending a contemnor to prison. But, if it does so think fit to act, it seems to me that all the safeguards required by the High Court must still be satisfied. The notice which is given to the accused must give with it the charges against him with all the particularity which this court or the High Court here ordinarily requires before depriving a person of his liberty. The accused must be given notice of any new charge and the opportunity of meeting it. Even if he does not appear to answer it, it must be proved with all the sufficiency which we habitually require before depriving a man of his liberty.

'Having analysed the evidence as it has been put before us in this case, I must say that it falls far short of that which we would require for such a purpose. In my opinion, therefore, the orders of committal should be set aside and the warrants should not be executed'.

3 The five dockers

Just over five weeks later, 26 July 1972, that story almost repeated itself. But this time it was five dockers, not three. They picketed the container depot. The Industrial Court ordered that they were to be imprisoned for contempt. Again there was the threat of a general strike. Again we were ready to hear an immediate appeal by the Official Solicitor. But he was told by someone to hold his hand. The reason was because the House of Lords rushed through a decision which was said to affect the matter. It was *Heaton's Case*[1]. They were busy amending their drafts – in typescript – right up to the last moment. Their decision was telephoned at once to the President of the Industrial Court. It gave him sufficient reason to revoke the order for committal. He revoked it. The general strike was averted. Another emergency was over.

The lesson to be learned from the dockers' cases is that the weapon of imprisonment should never be used – for contempt of court – in the case of industrial disputes. Some better means must be found. Can anyone suggest one?

1. [1973] AC 15.

4 The ward of court

Under this head of disobedience there are cases where a news-paper publishes a report of proceedings which are held in private. Most cases are — and are bound to be — heard in public and there is no bar to a fair and accurate report of them. But some cases are held in private: and a newspaper is guilty of a contempt of court if it publishes a report of what took place. Particularly is this the case in wardship proceedings which are usually held in private. The point arose in 1976 in a case reported as *Re F*[1]. A girl of 15 ran away with a man of 28. He gave her drugs and had sexual intercourse with her, knowing that she was only 15. Her parents were so worried that they applied for her to be made a ward of court. The girl was placed in a hostel. A social worker advised that the man of 28 should be allowed to visit her there. The *Daily Telegraph* got to know of this and published an article headed, 'Jailed lover "should visit hostel girl, 16" '.

The Official Solicitor thought that this article disclosed some of the proceedings which had taken place in private. He moved to commit the *Daily Telegraph* for contempt. The Judge held that it was a contempt. We reversed it. I said (at page 88):

'. . . . There are cases to show that it was a contempt of court of publish information relating to the *proceedings in court* about a ward. . . . The court was entitled to — and habitually did — hear the case in private. It could keep the proceedings away from the public gaze. The public were not admitted. Nor even the newspaper reporters. Only the parties, their legal advisers, and those immediately concerned were allowed in. When the court thus sat in private to hear ward-ship proceedings, the very sitting in private carried with it a prohibition forbidding publication of anything that took place, save only for the formal order made by the judge or an accurate summary of it: . . . .

1. [1977] Fam 58.

'A breach of that prohibition was considered a contempt of court. It was a criminal offence punishable by imprisonment. But what were the constituents of the offence? . . . .

'This kind of contempt is akin to the contempt which is committed by a person who disobeys an order of the court. Such as occurs where a party breaks an injunction ordering him to do something or to refrain from doing it. But there are differences between them. When one party breaks an injunction, it is the other party – the aggrieved person – who seeks to commit him for contempt. It is for his benefit that the injunction was granted, and for his benefit that it is enforced: . . . . The offender is not to be committed unless he has had proper notice of the terms of the injunction and it is proved, beyond reasonable doubt, that he has broken it: . . . . But when a newspaper editor – or anyone else for that matter – publishes information which relates to ward-ship proceedings, it is very different. He is no party to the proceedings. No order has been made against him. No notice has been given to him of any order made by the courts. He may – or may not – know whether the proceedings were in private or in open court. He may – or may not – be aware that there is a prohibition against publication. On what ground, therefore, is he to be found guilty? On what ground is he to be punished and sent to prison? What are the constituents of the offence?

'On principle, it seems to me that, in order to be found guilty the accused must have had a guilty mind – some guilty knowledge or intent – mens rea, as it is called. This question of mens rea often comes up. Much depends on the nature. "The mental elements of different crimes differ widely": . . . . What then is the mental element here? In considering it, it must be remembered that the offence is not restricted to newspaper editors or reporters. Anyone who publishes information relating to wardship proceedings may be found guilty. The girl herself, or her parents, or the lawyers in the case, may find themselves charged with the offence. Even if they only tell the story by word of mouth to a friend, they may be guilty of an offence: for that would be a publication

41

of it. Seeing that the offence is of such wide scope, it seems to me that a person is only to be found guilty of it if he has published information relating to wardship proceedings in circumstances in which he knows that publication is prohibited by law, or recklessly in circumstances in which he knows that the publication may be prohibited by law, but nevertheless goes on and publishes it, not caring whether it is prohibited, or not. As if he said: "I don't care whether it is forbidden, or not. I am not going to make any inquiries. I am going to publish it". Proof of this state of mind must be up to the standard required by the criminal law. It must be such as to leave no reasonable doubt outstanding.

'This test affords reasonable protection to ordinary folk, while, at the same time, it does not give a newspaper any freedom to publish information to the world at large. If a newspaper reporter knew that there were, or had recently been, wardship proceedings, he would be expected to know that they would be held in private and would know — or as good as know — that there was a prohibition against publication. Once he did know that there were, or had been, wardship proceedings, the prohibition would, I think, apply, not only to information given to the judge at the actual hearing, but also to confidential reports submitted beforehand by the Official Solicitor, or social workers, or the like.

'It remains to apply those principles to the newspapers in this case. The parents told the "Daily Telegraph" that the wardship order had been a temporary one and that it had expired. The newspaper thought that there was no longer any prohibition on publication. They made inquiry at the local council without getting any enlightenment. The "Evening Mail" made inquiries all round, including the Official Solicitor; and no one told them that the girl was a ward of court. Furthermore, both newspapers took the view that the matter was of such public interest that it should be brought to the notice of people in general — unless it was clearly prohibited by law. That was a legitimate view to take. They made inquiries. Finding no such prohibition, they published the information. In the circumstances, I do not think there was any guilty knowledge or intent on their part such as to warrant a finding that they were in contempt of court'.

6 Prejudicing a fair trial

1 'Vampire Arrested'

The freedom of the press is fundamental in our constitution. Newspapers have – and should have – the right to make fair comment on matters of public interest. But this is subject to the law of libel and of contempt of court. The newspapers must not make any comment which would tend to prejudice a fair trial. If they do, they will find themselves in trouble. The most spectacular case is one that is not reported in the Law Reports but which I remember well. Not that I usually read the newspapers much. Only *The Times* when it happens to appear. Its reports of legal decisions are unique. No other newspaper in the world has anything like it. They are written by barristers and are quoted in the Courts. But on this occasion the *Daily Mirror* went beyond all bounds. It came out with a banner headline – after a man called Haigh had been arrested and before he was charged –

'VAMPIRE ARRESTED'

It said that Haigh had been charged with one murder and had committed others and gave the names of persons who, it was said, he had murdered.

Lord Goddard was the Chief Justice. He said: 'There has been no more scandalous case. It is worthy of condign punishment'. He fined the newspaper £10,000. He sent the editor to prison for three months. He added: 'Let the directors beware. If this sort of thing should happen again, they may find that the arm of the law is strong enough to reach them too'.

2 The *Thalidomide case*

By far the most important case in recent years is the *Thalidomide case*. It is reported in the Court of Appeal in *AG v Times Newspapers Ltd* [1973] 1 QB 710 and in the House of Lords in [1974] AC 273. Mothers when pregnant had taken the drug thalidomide. Their children has been born deformed. That was in 1962. Actions were started at once for damages. Distillers, who distributed the drug, tried to settle the actions. All parents agreed to a settlement except five. An application was made to our Court to remove those five parents – as next friends – so as to get the children represented by the Official Solicitor. It was known that he would agree to a settlement. If that move had succeeded, all the cases would have been settled. There would have been no reported case anywhere. But we refused to remove those five parents. Our refusal is reported in *Re Taylor's Application*[1]. It was the turning point of the case. The rest is best told by what I said in the Court of Appeal[2] (at page 736):

'The editor of the "Sunday Times" tells us that the report of that case caused him great anxiety. Over 10 years had passed since the children were born with these deformities, and still no compensation had been paid by Distillers. He determined to investigate the matter in depth and to do all he could, through his newspaper, to persuade Distillers to take a fresh look at their moral responsibilities to all the thalidomide children, both those where writs had been issued and those where they had not. He had investigations made and launched a campaign against Distillers.

. . . .

'On 12 October 1972, the Attorney-General issued a writ against the "Sunday Times" claiming an injunction to restrain them from publishing the draft article.

. . . .

'It is undoubted law that, when litigation is pending and actively in suit before the court, no one shall comment on

1. [1972] 2 QB 369.
2. [1973] 1 QB 710.

45

it in such a way that there is a real and substantial danger of prejudice to the trial of the action, as for instance by influencing the judge, the jurors, or the witnesses, or even by prejudicing mankind in general against a party to the cause. That appears from the case before Lord Hardwicke LC in 1742 of *In re Read and Huggonson* (*St. James' Evening Post Case*) (1742) 2 Atk 469, and by many other cases to which the Attorney-General drew our attention. Even if the person making the comment honestly believes it to be true, still it is a contempt of court if he prejudges the truth before it is ascertained in the proceedings: see *Skipworth's Case* (1873) LR 9 QB 230, 234, by Blackburn J. To that rule about a fair trial, there is this further rule about bringing pressure to bear on a party: None shall, by misrepresentation or otherwise, bring unfair pressure to bear on one of the parties to a cause so as to force him to drop his complaint, or to give up his defence, or to come to a settlement on terms which he would not otherwise have been prepared to entertain. That appears from *In re William Thomas Shipping Co Ltd* [1930] 2 Ch 368 and *Vine Products Ltd v Green* [1966] Ch 484, to which I would add an article by Professor Goodhart on "Newspapers and Contempt of Court in English Law" in (1935) 48 *Harvard Law Review*, pp. 895, 896.

'I regard it as of the first importance that the law which I have just stated should be maintained in its full integrity. We must not allow "trial by newspaper" or "trial by television" or trial by any medium other than the courts of law.

'But in so stating the law, I would emphasise that it applies only "when litigation is pending and is actively in suit before the court". To which I would add that there must appear to be "a real and substantial danger of prejudice" to the trial of the case or to the settlement of it. And when considering the question, it must always be remembered that besides the interest of the parties in a fair trial or a fair settlement of the case there is another important interest to be considered. It is the interest of the public in matters of national concern, and the freedom of the press to make fair comment on such matters. The one interest must be balanced against the other.

There may be cases where the subject matter is such that the public interest counterbalances the private interest of the parties. In such cases the public interest prevails. Fair comment is to be allowed. It has been so stated in Australia in regard to the courts of law: see *Ex parte Bread Manufacturers Ltd* (1937) 37 SR (NSW) 242 and *Ex parte Dawson* [1961] SR (NSW) 573. It was so recommended by a committee presided over by Lord Salmon on *The Law of Contempt in Relation to Tribunals of Inquiry*: see (1969) Cmnd. 4078, para 26.

'Take this present case. Here we have a matter of the greatest public interest. The thalidomide children are the living reminders of a national tragedy. There has been no public inquiry as to how it came about. Such inquiry as there has been has been done in confidence in the course of private litigation between the parties. The compensation offered is believed by many to be too small. Nearly 12 years have passed and still no settlement has been reached. On such a matter the law can and does authorise the newspapers to make fair comment. So long as they get their facts right, and keep their comments fair, they are without reproach. They do not offend against the law as to contempt of court unless there is real and substantial prejudice to pending litigation which is actively in suit before the court. Our law of contempt does not prevent comment before the litigation is started, nor after it has ended. Nor does it prevent it when the litigation is dormant and is not being actively pursued. If the pending action is one which, as a matter of public interest, ought to have been brought to trial long ago, or ought to have been settled long ago, the newspapers can fairly comment on the failure to bring it to trial or to reach a settlement. No person can stop comment by serving a writ and letting it lie idle: nor can he stop it by entering an appearance and doing nothing more. It is active litigation which is protected by the law of contempt, not the absence of it.

'Apply these considerations to the present case. Take the first 62 actions which were settled in February 1968. The newspapers can fairly comment on those settlements, saying that in making them the Distillers company did not measure up to their moral responsibilities. Take the last 123 children in regard to whom writs have never been issued. The newspapers can fairly press for compensation on the ground that Distillers were morally responsible. That leaves only the 266 actions in which writs were issued four years ago but have never been brought to trial. Does the existence of those writs prevent the newspapers from drawing attention to the moral responsibilities of Distillers? If they can comment on the first 62 or the last 123, I do not see why they cannot comment on these intervening 266. There is no way of distinguishing between them. The draft article comments on all the thalidomide children together. It is clearly lawful in respect of the first 62 and the last 123. So also it should be in respect of the middle 266.

'I have said enough to show that this case is unique. So much so that in my opinion the public interest in having it discussed outweighs the prejudice which might thereby be occasioned to a party to the dispute. At any rate, the High Court of Parliament has allowed it to be discussed. So why should not we in these courts also permit it? There is no possible reason why Parliament should permit it and we refuse it'.

Our decision was reversed by the House of Lords. I hope that I will be forgiven for not quoting from their judgments. They stated a new principle. It was that newspapers should not publish comments or articles which 'prejudged the issue in pending proceedings'. This new principle was criticised by the Committee over which our dear friend Lord Justice Phillimore presided[1]. It was a very good Committee. 'Harry' Phillimore, as we knew him affectionately, devoted his last years to it. They heard much evidence and disposed of the House of Lords by saying (at page 48):

'The simple test of prejudgment therefore seems to go too

1. (1974) Cmnd. 5794.

far in some respects and not far enough in others. We conclude that no satisfactory definition can be found which does not have direct reference to the mischief which the law of contempt is and always has been designed to suppress. That mischief is the risk of prejudice to the due administration of justice'.

Hitherto we have always expected a decision of the House of Lords to be final and conclusive. But the *Thalidomide case* showed the contrary. The *Sunday Times* took it to the European Court of Human Rights. They relied on Article 10 of the European Convention to which the United Kingdom has adhered. It says that:

'Everyone has the right to freedom of expression. This right shall include freedom to hold opinions and to receive and impart information and ideas without interference by public authority and regardless of frontiers'.

The European Court of Human Rights, by a majority of 11 to 9, upheld the claim of the *Sunday Times*. It had a right to impart information about the *Thalidomide case*. Inferentially they thought that the House of Lords were wrong and that the Court of Appeal were right. Three cheers for the European Court. But what will the House of Lords do now? Will they still regard themselves as infallible? They have Francis Mann on their side, see *The Law Quarterly Review* for July 1979, pp. 348–354.

3 A 'gagging writ'

Let us hope too that the public interest will prevail so as to stop what has been called a 'gagging writ'. There was a company director called Wallersteiner. He tried to stop criticism of him at a shareholders' meeting. He issued a writ against the complaining shareholder: and then sought to shut him up by saying the matter was 'sub judice'. I dealt with this once and for all, I hope, in *Wallersteiner v Moir*[1]:

1. [1974] 1 WLR 991 at 1004–1005.

'I know that it is commonly supposed that once a writ is issued, it puts a stop to discussion. If anyone wishes to canvass the matter in the press or in public, it cannot be permitted. It is said to be "sub judice". I venture to suggest that is a complete misconception. The sooner it is corrected, the better. If it is a matter of public interest, it can be discussed at large without fear of thereby being in contempt of court. Criticisms can continue to be made and can be repeated. Fair comment does not prejudice a fair trial. That was well pointed out by Salmon J in *Thomson v Times Newspapers Ltd* [1969] 1 WLR 1236, 1239–1240. The law says — and says emphatically — that the issue of a writ is not to be used so as to be a muzzle to prevent discussion. Jacob Factor tried to suppress the "Daily Mail" on that score, but failed: see *R v Daily Mail (Editor), ex parte Factor* (1928) 44 TLR 303. And Lord Reid has said that a "gagging writ" ought to have no effect: see *Attorney-General v Times Newspapers Ltd* [1974] AC 273, 301. Matters of public interest should be, and are, open to discussion, notwithstanding the issue of a writ.

'So here I would hold that a discussion of company affairs at a company meeting is not a contempt of court. Even if a writ has been issued and those affairs are the subject of litigation, the discussion of them cannot be stopped by the magic words "sub judice". It may be there are newspaper reporters present — so that the words will be published at large next day. Nevertheless, the shareholders can discuss the company affairs quite freely without fear of offending the court. The reason is simple. Such discussion does not prejudice fair trial of the action. No judge is likely to read the newspaper reports, let alone be influenced by them. Nor are the members of a jury, if there should be a jury. They do not read the reports of company meetings. In any case, they would not remember them by the time of the trial. Mr. Lincoln suggested that someone at the meeting might use words such as to bring improper pressure to bear on the litigants or on witnesses. If that were so, I have no doubt the court could intervene. But that suggestion cannot be admitted as an excuse for stifling discussion. And Lord Reid said in *Attorney-General v Times Newspapers Ltd* [1974] AC 273, 296: "there must be a balancing of relevant considerations". The most weighty consideration is the public interest. The shareholders of a public company should be free to discuss the company affairs at the company meetings. If a shareholder feels that there have been, or may be, abuses by those in control of the company, he should be at liberty to give voice to them.

'I can well see, of course, that this freedom of discussion must not be carried too far. It must not deteriorate into disorder. The chairman must control the meeting. He must keep order. After time enough has been allowed, he can bring the discussion to a close. If his own conduct is under fire, he could vacate the chair, and allow it to be taken by another. If these rules are observed, there should be no trouble'.

4 The Exclusive Brethren

There remains one last point. Which are the courts to be protected by the law of contempt? Hitherto the question has arisen in regard to the superior courts. But do the same principles apply to the inferior courts? We had to consider it recently when a case was pending in a local valuation court about rates. It is *Attorney-General v British Broadcasting Corporation*[1]. A religious sect sought to stop a television broadcast which was disparaging of them. It all depended if the Local Valuation Court was a 'court' which the law would protect. My colleagues thought it was. I thought it was not. I ventured to summarise the principles in these words:

'How far do these principles apply to the inferior courts? I pause to say that the word "inferior" is a misdescription. They are not inferior in the doing of justice: nor in the judges who man them: nor in the advocates who plead in them. They are called "inferior" only because they try cases of a

1. [1979] 3 WLR 312 at 319.

lesser order of importance — as it is thought. But the cases which they try are often of equal concern to the parties and the public. I see no reason whatever why the principles which have been evolved for the superior courts should not apply equally to the inferior courts. The stream of justice should be kept pure and clear in all the courts, superior and inferior, alike. That is the way in which the law seems to be developing, as is shown by the cases on contempt of court: . . . and the cases on the liability of judges: . . . and on absolute privilege of advocate and witness:. . . . The only qualification is in the manner of enforcing those principles. Where there is contempt of court, if it comes to granting injunctions or inflicting penalties, this is left to the superior courts: . . . . But otherwise the principles should be the same for all.

'But the principles — which confer immunity and protection — have hitherto been confined to the well-recognised courts, in which I include, of course, not only the High Court, but also the Crown Court, the county courts, the magistrates' courts, the consistory courts and courts-martial. The principles have not hitherto been extended to the newly established courts, of which we have so many. The answer cannot depend on whether the word "court" appears in the title. There are many newly formed bodies which go by the name of "tribunal" but which have all the characteristics of the recognised courts, such as the industrial tribunals, and the solicitors' disciplinary tribunal. To my mind, the immunities and protections which are accorded to the recognised courts of the land should be extended to all tribunals or bodies which have equivalent characteristics. After all, if the principles are good for the old, so they should be good for the new. I would, therefore, be venturesome. I would suggest that the immunities and protections should be extended to all tribunals set up by or under the authority of Parliament or of the Crown which exercise equivalent functions by equivalent procedures and are manned by equivalent personnel as those of the recognised courts of the land: . . . .

'Applying this test, I would suggest that commercial arbitrations are excluded because they are not set up by or under the authority of Parliament or of the Crown. Planning inquiries are excluded because their function is not to hear and determine, but only to inquire and report. Licensing bodies are excluded because they exercise administrative functions and not judicial: . . . . Assessment committees are excluded because they are manned by laymen and not by lawyers. And so on.

'What then about a local valuation court? It is the successor of the old assessment committees, which are certainly not courts: . . . .

'In any case, to my mind this body lacks one important characteristic of a court. It has no one on it or connected with it who is legally qualified or experienced. To constitute a court there should be a chairman who is a lawyer or at any rate who has at his elbow a clerk or assistant who is a lawyer qualified by examination or by experience, as a justices' clerk is. The reason is that a lawyer is, or should be, by his training and experience better able than others to keep to the relevant and exclude the irrelevant; to decide according to the evidence adduced and not be influenced by outside information; to interpret the words of statutes or regulations as Parliament intended; to have recourse to legal books of reference and be able to consult them; and generally to know how the proceedings of a court should be conducted.

'It is for this reason that it is my opinion that the local valuation court is not a court properly so called. . .'.

My two colleagues differed from me. They held it was a court: but they agreed with me on a more important matter. In the case of a civil action which is to be tried by a judge, it is very rare indeed that a newspaper would be guilty of contempt by making comments on it. As I said (at page 319):

'No professionally trained judge would be influenced by anything he read in the newspapers or saw on television'.

Conclusion

Looking at it broadly, the process of Contempt of Court is designed to secure that every person has a fair trial; or, to put it in other words, it is a procedure by which the Court condemns any conduct which tends to prejudice a fair trial. The Courts will restrain it by injunction beforehand or by punishment afterwards. The present tendency is to say that the process should be left in the hands of the Attorney-General: that he is the person who should decide whether it should be invoked or not. It is no doubt proper for any complaint to be laid before the Attorney-General so that he may, if he thinks fit, institute proceedings for contempt. But it should not be exclusively in his hands. Some cases wear a political complexion. The Attorney-General may be reluctant to take proceedings for fear of repercussions affecting his party. So the Courts should be able to take steps at the instance of anyone who has a sufficient interest in the matter.

Part two

Inquiries into conduct

Introduction

Many of the questions of the day are not decided in the courts of law or even in judicial tribunals. The issues are not 'justiciable' as the phrase goes. They are entrusted to commissions of inquiry, to inspectors, licensing bodies and the like. Not being justiciable, they are not subject to appeal to Courts of Law: and there may be no remedy given by statute. But it is very important that their proceedings should be conducted fairly. To this end, the Courts have evolved processes by which to control them. Especially as on some occasions these bodies may make findings or come to conclusions very adverse to the individual. They may not be subject to mandamus or certiorari. Yet in one way or another the Courts have evolved machinery to deal with them. To this I now turn.

I must however first deal with the Judges themselves. They too are not perfect. They may make mistakes and thereby do injustice. You may remember the parable of the unjust 'judge who feared not God, neither regarded man'. He decided in favour of the widow 'lest by her continual coming she weary me' (St. Luke 18: 2–5). Can such an injustice be corrected by anyone? In many cases a mistake of a judge can be corrected on appeal. But some mistakes cannot. These may be due to ignorance or incompetence or bias or even malice. They may put litigants to much expense, anxiety and damage. In most other professions, negligence may give rise to an action for damages. Is a judge exempt when other professional men are liable? Ought he not to insure himself (or the Government insure him) against his mistakes? What is the reason behind his immunity?

1 Into the conduct of judges

1 The judge who talked too much

Once upon a time there was a judge who talked too much. He asked too many questions. One after another in quick succession. Of witnesses in the box. Of counsel in their submissions. So much so that they counted up the number. His exceeded all the rest put together. Both counsel made it a ground of appeal.

He was The Honourable Sir Hugh Imbert Periam Hallett whose initials gave him the nickname 'Hippy' Hallett. He had been a judge for 17 years. He earned a big reputation as a junior at the bar: and in silk for his knowledge of the law. He used to appear in the Privy Council where Lord Maugham appreciated his talents and appointed him a judge in 1939. He started his judicial career quietly enough but – as often happens – as his experience grew so did his loquacity. He got so interested in every case that he dived deep into every detail of it. He became a byword.

The climax came in an ordinary sort of case. It is *Jones v National Coal Board*[1]. The roof of a coal-mine had fallen in. A miner had been buried by it and died. The widow claimed damages. The case was tried by Hallett J at Chester. He rejected the widow's claim. She appealed on the ground, among others, that the Judge's interruptions had made it impossible for her counsel to put her case properly. The Board put in a cross-appeal including among others that the Judge's interruptions had prevented the Board from having

1. [1957] 2 QB 55.

58

a fair trial. The appeal was argued before us by Mr. Gerald
Gardiner QC (afterwards Lord Chancellor) for the widow. He
was the most able advocate I have known. On the other side
side Mr. Edmund Davies QC (afterwards Lord Edmund-
Davies). He was the most resourceful. We usually in such a
case give judgment straightaway at the end of the argument.
But on this occasion we reserved it for just over three weeks.
We realised that it might lead to the end of the Judge's career;
as it did. So we took special care. This is what I said, speaking
for the whole Court[1]:

'We much regret that it has fallen to our lot to consider such
a complaint against one of Her Majesty's judges: but consider
it we must, because we can only do justice between these
parties if we are satisfied that the primary facts have been
properly found by the judge on a fair trial between the
parties. Once we have the primary facts fairly found, we are
in as good a position as the judge to draw inferences or
conclusions from those facts, but we cannot embark on this
task unless the foundation of primary facts is secure.
. . . .
'No one can doubt that the judge, in intervening as he
did, was actuated by the best motives. He was anxious to
understand the details of this complicated case, and asked
questions to get them clear in his mind. He was anxious
that the witnesses should not be harassed unduly in crossexamination, and intervened to protect them when he
thought necessary. He was anxious to investigate all the
various criticisms that had been made against the board, and
to see whether they were well founded or not. Hence, he
took them up himself with the witnesses from time to time.
He was anxious that the case should not be dragged on too
long, and intimated clearly when he thought that a point
had been sufficiently explored. All those are worthy motives
on which judges daily intervene in the conduct of cases, and
have done for centuries.

1. Ibid. at 61.

'Nevertheless, we are quite clear that the interventions, taken together, were far more than they should have been. In the system of trial which we have evolved in this country, the judge sits to hear and determine the issues raised by the parties, not to conduct an investigation or examination on behalf of society at large, as happens, we believe, in some foreign countries. Even in England, however, a judge is not a mere umpire to answer the question "How's that?" His object, above all, is to find out the truth, and to do justice according to law; and in the daily pursuit of it the advocate plays an honourable and necessary role. Was it not Lord Eldon LC who said in a notable passage that "truth is best discovered by powerful statements on both sides of the question"?: see *Ex parte Lloyd*[1]. And Lord Greene MR who explained that justice is best done by a judge who holds the balance between the contending parties without himself taking part in their disputations? If a judge, said Lord Greene, should himself conduct the examination of witnesses, "he, so to speak, descends into the arena and is liable to have his vision clouded by the dust of conflict": see *Yuill v Yuill*[2].

'Yes, he must keep his vision unclouded. It is all very well to paint justice blind, but she does better without a bandage round her eyes. She should be blind indeed to favour or prejudice, but clear to see which way lies the truth: and the less dust there is about the better. Let the advocates one after the other put the weights into the scales — the "nicely calculated less or more" — but the judge at the end decides which way the balance tilts, be it ever so slightly. So firmly is all this established in our law that the judge is not allowed in a civil dispute to call a witness whom he thinks might throw some light on the facts. He must rest content with the witnesses called by the parties: see *In re Enoch & Zaretzky, Bock & Co*[3]. So also it is for the advocates, each in his turn, to examine the witnesses, and not for the judge to take it on himself lest by so doing he appear to favour one side or

1. (1822) Mont 70 at 72n.
2. [1945] P 15 at 20, [1945] 1 All ER 183, 61 TLR 176.
3. [1910] 1 KB 327.

the other: see *R v Cain*[1], *R v Bateman*[2], and *Harris v Harris*[3], by Birkett LJ especially. And it is for the advocate to state his case as fairly and strongly as he can, without undue interruption, lest the sequence of his argument be lost: see *R v Clewer*[4]. The judge's part in all this is to hearken to the evidence, only himself asking questions of witnesses when it is necessary to clear up any point that has been overlooked or left obscure; to see that the advocates behave themselves seemly and keep to the rules laid down by law; to exclude irrelevancies and discourage repetition; to make sure by wise intervention that he follows the points that the advocates are making and can assess their worth; and at the end to make up his mind where the truth lies. If he goes beyond this, he drops the mantle of a judge and assumes the robe of an advocate; and the change does not become him well. Lord Chancellor Bacon spoke right when he said that[5]: "Patience and gravity of hearing is an essential part of justice; and an over-speaking judge is no well-tuned cymbal".

'Such are our standards. They are set so high that we cannot hope to attain them all the time. In the very pursuit of justice, our keenness may outrun our sureness, and we may trip and fall. That is what has happened here. A judge of acute perception, acknowledged learning, and actuated by the best of motives, has nevertheless himself intervened so much in the conduct of the case that one of the parties — nay, each of them — has come away complaining that he was not able properly to put his case; and these complaints are, we think, justified.

. . . .

'In these circumstances, we think we must grant the widow a new trial. There is one thing to which everyone in this country is entitled, and that is a fair trial at which he can put his case properly before the judge. The widow and the National Coal Board stand in this respect on the level. No

1. (1936) 25 Cr App Rep 204.
2. (1946) 31 Cr App Rep 106.
3. (1952), *Times*, 9 April; Judgments of the Court of Appeal, 1952, No. 148.
4. (1953) 37 Cr App Rep 37.
5. *Essays or Counsels Civil and Moral:* 'Of Judicature'.

cause is lost until the judge has found it so; and he cannot find it without a fair trial, nor can we affirm it'.

At that time Lord Kilmuir was Lord Chancellor. Of course he did not speak to me of the case beforehand, but afterwards he told me that he was grateful to us. He sent for the Judge. It was arranged that he should continue to sit for a little while and then resign. That he did at the end of the summer term. It was a poignant case; for he was able and intelligent — but he asked too many questions.

After that case, there were several appeals which came before us — from other judges — on similar grounds. The lawyers used to get the shorthand notes, count up the number of questions asked by the judge and by counsel, and then ask for a new trial. But I do not remember any appeal that succeeded on that ground. 'Hippy' Hallett stands in isolation. Let others take heed.

2 The judge who made a mistake

In that case the mistake of the judge gave rise to a new trial and caused much expense to the parties. No one would dream of making the judge personally liable for such an innocent mistake. But suppose a judge makes a mistake owing to a misunderstanding; and as a result a man is wrongly detained in prison. Can the judge be made liable in damages? The point arose in *Sirros v Moore*[1].

Sirros was a Turk. He was given leave to come into England as a visitor. He overstayed his leave. The magistrate recommended him for deportation and meanwhile directed that he *be not detained*. Sirros appealed to the Crown Court against the recommendation for deportation. His appeal was heard by a circuit judge and two magistrates. Sirros went into the Appeal Court a free man. He had a solicitor's clerk with him. He asked that the recommendation be reversed. The judge dismissed his appeal. So in due course Sirros would be

1. [1974] 3 WLR 459.

deported; but pending deportation, he was not to be detained. He was still entitled to go free. But the judge cannot have realised this. He must have thought that Sirros was already in custody. Then this happened (page 464):

'. . . . The judge then announced his decision: "The appeal is dismissed". Thereupon Sirros and the solicitor's clerk got up from their seats and made their way out of the court. The case was to all appearances over. After a little while, the judge looked up. He saw Sirros leaving the court: or rather he saw the back of his head disappearing. A minute or two later the judge called out "Stop him". Police officers hurried out after him. But he had gone. He went out of the court building in St. James's Square. He got as far as Jermyn Street: but then Sergeant Moore and other police officers caught him and brought him back. He was put in the cells. The judge meanwhile had gone to lunch.

. . . .

'On the judge's return, counsel submitted that Sirros should not be detained, and he asked for bail. He called witnesses as to his character. It took about an hour. The judge refused to grant bail. So Sirros was taken away in custody.

. . . .

'On the very next day, Sirros's counsel applied for a writ of habeas corpus. . . .

'The Divisional Court ordered that a writ of habeas corpus was to be issued. So he went free. Ashworth J said:
"On one matter I have no doubt whatever, and that is that the detention of this applicant was wholly unauthorised. . .".

'Ten days later, Sirros issued a writ against the judge and the police officers claiming damages for assault and false imprisonment. He specified two things against the judge: (1) the order to "stop him" in the morning; (2) the order in the afternoon when the judge refused to grant bail, thus continuing the detention. He claimed against the police officers as acting on the judge's orders'.

Those facts raised distinctly the question whether a judge

could be made liable for making a mistake — which he ought not to have made if he had been taking proper care. No such case had arisen for 100 years or more. Sirros's case was taken up by one of our new law centres for helping the poor. It was the North Kensington Law Centre; and they instructed Lord Gifford. His great-grandfather was Master of the Rolls 155 years ago but he is still a junior who takes up cases for the poor. The judge was represented by the Treasury Devil, Mr. Gordon Slynn. As you might expect, it was well argued on both sides. Then we sought to state the modern position (page 467):

'Ever since the year 1613, if not before, it has been accepted in our law that no action is maintainable against a judge for anything said or done by him in the exercise of a jurisdiction which belongs to him. The words which he speaks are protected by an absolute privilege. The orders which he gives, and the sentences which he imposes, cannot be made the subject of civil proceedings against him. No matter that the judge was under some gross error or ignorance, or was actuated by envy, hatred and malice, and all uncharitableness, he is not liable to an action. The remedy of the party aggrieved is to appeal to a Court of Appeal or to apply for habeas corpus, or a writ of error or certiorari, or take some such step to reverse his ruling. Of course, if the judge has accepted bribes or been in the least degree corrupt, or has perverted the course of justice, he can be punished in the criminal courts. That apart, however, a judge is not liable to an action for damages. The reason is not because the judge has any privilege to make mistakes or to do wrong. It is so that he should be able to do his duty with complete independence and free from fear. It was well stated by Lord Tenterden CJ in *Garnett v Ferrand* (1827) 6 B & C 611, 625: "This freedom from action and question at the suit of an individual is given by the law to the judges, not so much for their own sake as for the sake of the public, and for the advancement of justice, that being free from actions, they may be free in thought and independent in judgment, as all who are to administer justice ought to be".

'Those words apply not only to judges of the superior courts, but to judges of all ranks, high or low. . . .

. . . .

'In the old days, as I have said, there was a sharp distinction between the inferior courts and the superior courts. Whatever may have been the reason for this distinction, it is no longer valid. There has been no case on the subject for the last one hundred years at least. And during this time our judicial system has changed out of all knowledge. So great is this change that it is now appropriate for us to reconsider the principles which should be applied to judicial acts. In this new age I would take my stand on this: as a matter of principle the judges of superior courts have no greater claim to immunity than the judges of the lower courts. Every judge of the courts of this land – from the highest to the lowest – should be protected to the same degree, and liable to the same degree. If the reason underlying this immunity is to ensure "that they may be free in thought and independent in judgment", it applies to every judge, whatever his rank. Each should be protected from liability to damages when he is acting judicially. Each should be able to do his work in complete independence and free from fear. He should not have to turn the pages of his books with trembling fingers, asking himself: "If I do this, shall I be liable in damages?" So long as he does his work in the honest belief that it is within his jurisdiction, then he is not liable to an action. He may be mistaken in fact. He may be ignorant in law. What he does may be outside his jurisdiction – in fact or in law – but so long as he honestly believes it to be within his jurisdiction, he should not be liable. Once he honestly entertains this belief, nothing else will make him liable. He is not to be plagued with allegations of malice or ill-will or bias or anything of the kind. Actions based on such allegations have been struck out and will continue to be struck out. Nothing will make him liable except it be shown that he was not acting judicially, knowing that he had no jurisdiction to do it.

'This principle should cover the justices of the peace also. They should no longer be subject to "strokes of the rodde, or spur". Aided by their clerks, they do their work with the highest degree of responsibility and competence — to the satisfaction of the entire community. They should have the same protection as the other judges.

. . . .

'The judge had no jurisdiction to detain Sirros in custody. The Divisional Court were right to release him on habeas corpus. Though the judge was mistaken, yet he acted judicially and for that reason no action will lie against him. Likewise, no action will lie against the police officers. They are protected in respect of anything they did at his direction, not knowing it was wrong: . . .'.

2 Into the conduct of ministers

So much for a judge when he is acting as a judge. But there are times when a judge is invited by the Government of the day to undertake an inquiry or to chair a committee. He has then no special privilege or immunity. So it behoves him to act with circumspection. The Government usually asks a judge to do such a task when it is in a quandary. There is public unease: and the only person who can be trusted to be impartial is a judge. He is independent of the executive: and thus can speak his mind.

Thus I was called upon in June 1963. The Government was indeed in a quandary. The Secretary of State for War, The Rt. Hon. John Profumo, OBE, had resigned during the Whitsun recess. The *Sunday Mirror* had published a photographic copy of his letter to Christine Keeler. It started 'Darling' and ended 'Love J'. The newspaper had paid her for it. Rumours spread like wildfire. Not only about Mr. Profumo and the Russian Naval Attaché. But many other ministers also. Their morale was shaken to the core. The security of the realm was said to be endangered. Nothing like it has been seen since Titus Oates spread his lies in 1678 when Macaulay tells us 'the capital and the whole nation was mad with hatred and fear'. The members of the House of Commons held a debate on Monday, 17 June 1963. On the Friday, 21 June 1963, the Prime Minister (Mr. Harold Macmillan) asked me to inquire into the security situation. Some have since said that, as a judge, I should not have accepted the task – because of its political overtones. But I felt, and still feel, that when the security of the State was

67

involved, it was my duty to do what I was asked. I still have a copy of my reply on 24 June 1963:

'Dear Prime Minister,

It is a great responsibility with which you have entrusted me — and I feel very apprehensive of my ability to carry it out. All I can say is that I will do my very best faithfully to perform the task.

Yours sincerely,

Denning'.

As it was so urgent and important, I put everything else aside. I did it alone. Just two secretaries and two shorthand-writers. I had a room in the Treasury in Whitehall. There I saw Ministers of the Crown, the Security Service, rumour-mongers and prostitutes. They all came in by back doors and along corridors secretly so that the newspapers should not spot them. Some of the evidence I heard was so disgusting — even to my sophisticated mind — that I sent the lady shorthand-writers out and had no note of it taken. On one occasion the photographers were allowed in to see me at work. I kept them at a far distance so that they should not see what I was writing. Afterwards they blew up the photograph and published me writing a letter 'Dear Minister'. They accused me — the guardian of security — of lack of proper care in security. 'Quis custodiet ipsos custodes' — who will guard the guards themselves? (Afterwards they were rebuked by the Press Council.) One young lady, Mandy Rice-Davies, said to the newspapers, 'Quite the nicest Judge I have ever met'.

Every weekend I went home and worked there on the papers. Invariably the journalists arrived with photographers. On the day when I made my report, a score or more of them were on our country station. They took photographs showing the chickens on the platform. They travelled up in the same train. Independent television made a film about me with the refrain running through, 'Onward, Christian soldiers'.

If you are interested in the story itself, you can read it all in my Report of 16 September 1963. It was a best-seller. The

Daily Telegraph published it in full as a supplement to their paper. There were queues at the Stationery Office wanting to buy it. Right up till midnight. It became a common joke that 'B.C.' and 'A.D.' stood for 'Before Christine' and 'After Denning'.

But, for those of the new generation who will not have read the Report, I will set out the principles on which I conducted the inquiry[1]:

'It has been much debated what is the best way to deal with matters such as those referred to me. The appointment of a tribunal under the Tribunal of Inquiries Act 1921 is an elaborate and costly machine, equipped with all the engines of the law – counsel, solicitors, witnesses on oath, absolute privilege, openness to the public (so far as possible) and committal for contempt – but it suffers from the invincible drawback, in doing justice, that there is no prosecution, no charge, and no defence. The appointment of a Select Committee of one or both Houses of Parliament is a very representative body, but it is said to suffer from the draw-back (to some eyes) that the inquisitors are too many and may be influenced in their, often divergent, views by political considerations, so that there may be too much dissent to carry authority. Now there is this inquiry which I have been entrusted with *alone*. It has the advantage that there can be no dissent, but it has two great disadvantages: first, being in secret, it has not the appearance of justice; second, in carrying out the inquiry, I have had to be detective, inquisitor, advo-cate and judge, and it has been difficult to combine them. But I have come to see that it has three considerable advan-tages. First, inasmuch as it has been held in private and in strict confidence, the witnesses were, I am sure, much more frank than they would otherwise have been. Secondly, I was able to check the evidence of one witness against that of another more freely. Thirdly, and most important, aspersions cast by witnesses against others (who are not able to defend themselves) do not achieve the publicity which is inevitable in a Court of Law or Tribunal of Inquiry.

'You were good enough to say that, if I needed further powers, I was to ask for them. I have not felt the need. Every witness whom I asked to come, has come, without being subpoenaed. Every witness has answered the questions I put to him, without being threatened with contempt. I have been told as much truth without an oath as if it were on oath. It was not the lack of powers which handicapped me. It was the very nature of the inquiry with which I was entrusted.

'At every stage of this inquiry I have been faced with this great anxiety: How far should I go into matters which seem to show that someone or other has been guilty of a criminal offence, or of professional misconduct, or moral turpitude, or even incompetence? My inquiry is not a suitable body to determine guilt or innocence. I have not the means at my disposal. No witness has given evidence on oath. None has been crossexamined. No charge has been preferred. No opportunity to defend has been open. It poses for me an inescapable dilemma: *On the one hand*, if I refrain from going into such matters, my inquiry will be thwarted. Questions that have been asked in the public interest will not be answered. Suspicions that have already fallen heavily on innocent persons may not be removed. Yet, *on the other hand*, if I do go into these matters I may well place persons under a cloud when it is undeserved: and I may impute to them offences or misconduct which they have never had the chance to rebut. Above all I have to remember that the information that I have been given has been given in confidence. In order to enable every witness to speak frankly and truly to me, I have assured each one that what they tell me is in strict confidence and will be used only for the purposes of my inquiry and report. This means that, whatever I say in this report, it should not be used for any other purpose: in particular none of it should be used for the purposes of any prosecution or proceeding against anyone. But I cannot, of course, prevent anyone from seeking evidence *aliunde* and acting on it.

'Such being the inescapable difficulties inherent in this form of inquiry, I have come to the conclusion that all I can do is this:

'When the facts are clear beyond controversy, I will state them as objectively as I can, irrespective of the consequences to individuals: and I will draw any inference that is manifest from those facts. But when the facts are in issue, I must always remember the cardinal principle of justice — that no man is to be condemned on suspicion. There must be evidence which proves his guilt before he is pronounced to be so. I will therefore take the facts in his favour rather than do an injustice which is without remedy. For from my findings there is no appeal.

'To those who in consequence will reproach me for "whitewashing", I would make this answer: While the public interest demands that the facts should be ascertained as completely as possible, there is a yet higher public interest to be considered, namely, the interest of justice to the individual which overrides all other. At any rate, speaking as a Judge, I put justice first'.

Next I will set out one sentence in which I reached my conclusion, adverse, I fear, to the Prime Minister and his colleagues (para. 286):

'. . . . It was the responsibility of the Prime Minister and his colleagues, and of them only, to deal with this situation: and they did not succeed in doing so'.

Finally, in my conclusion I dealt with the rumours which had caused so much disturbance in the country (paras. 339–343):

'I know that Ministers and others have felt so aggrieved by the rumours about them that they have contemplated bringing actions for libel or slander in respect of them. I know, too, that they have refrained from doing so pending my inquiry. I hope, however, that they will not feel that honour requires them to pursue these matters further. My findings will, I trust, be accepted by them as a full and sufficient vindication

71

of their good names. It is, I believe, better for the country that these rumours should be buried and that this unfortunate episode should be closed.

'Equally I trust that all others will now cease to repeat these rumours which have been proved so unfounded and untrue: and that newspapers and others will not seek to put names to those whom I have deliberately left anonymous. For I fear that, if names are given, human nature being what it is, people will say "there's no smoke without fire" — a proposition which in this instance is demonstrably untrue.

'This brings me to the end. It might be thought — indeed it has been thought — by some that these rumours are a symptom of a decline in the integrity of public life in this country. I do not believe this to be true. There has been no lowering of standards. But there is this difference today. Public men are more vulnerable than they were: and it behoves them, even more than ever, to give no cause for scandal. For if they do, they have to reckon with a growing hazard which has been disclosed in the evidence I have heard. Scandalous information about well-known people has become a marketable commodity. True or false, actual or invented, it can be sold. The greater the scandal the higher the price it commands. If supported by photographs or letters, real or imaginary, all the better. Often enough the sellers profess to have been themselves participants in the discreditable conduct which they seek to exploit. Intermediaries move in, ready to assist the sale and ensure the highest prices. The story improves with the telling. It is offered to those newspapers — there are only a few of them — who deal in this commodity. They vie with one another to buy it. Each is afraid the other will get it first. So they buy it on chance that it will turn out profitable. Sometimes it is no use to them. It is palpably false. At other times it is credible. But even so, they dare not publish the whole of the information. The law of libel and the rules of contempt of court exert an effective restraint. They publish what they can, but there remains a substantial part which is not fit for publication. This unpublished part goes round by word of mouth. It does not stop in Fleet Street. It goes to Westminster. It crosses the

Channel, even the Atlantic and back again, swelling all the time. Yet without the original purchase, it might never have got started on its way.

'When such deplorable consequences are seen to ensue, the one thing that is clear is that something should be done to stop the trafficking in scandal for reward. The machinery is ready to hand. There is a new Press Council already in being.

'Although I have felt it necessary to draw attention to this matter, I would like to say that I have had the greatest cooperation and assistance from the newspapers and all concerned with them; and not least from those whose practices I hold to be open to criticism'.

Following the Report, Mr. Harold Macmillan fell ill; and resigned. Sir Alec Douglas-Home became Prime Minister. There was a debate on 16 December 1963 in the House of Commons on 'Security and the Denning Report'. In the course of it Mr. Harold Macmillan said[1]:

'This debate takes place in circumstances very different, as far as I personally am concerned, from what I had envisaged up to two months ago, ... I wished to express publicly what I have, of course, expressed privately, my gratitude to Lord Denning for undertaking the delicate and difficult task which I asked him to perform. I am sure that that is the universal view in the House and in the country'.

Later on it was made clear that there ought never to be an inquiry like it again. A Royal Commission on Tribunals of Inquiry under the Chairmanship of Lord Justice Salmon, reporting in 1966, made this comment[2]:

'Lord Denning's Report[3] was generally accepted by the public. But this was only because of Lord Denning's rare qualities and high reputation. Even so, the public acceptance of the Report may be regarded as a brilliant exception to what would normally occur when an inquiry is carried out under such conditions'.

1. 686 HC Official Report (5th Series), col. 911 (16 December 1963).
2. Cmnd. 3121, para. 21.
3. Cmnd. 2152.

3 Into the conduct of directors

1 Behind the curtain

Our system of company law has only been in existence for some 120 years. It is the universal medium of business. Most merchants and most traders are now limited liability companies. Not only in England but also in countries overseas. The law, however, has let down a curtain which conceals the goings on of the directors and managers of a company. Beneath this curtain all sorts of fraud can be perpetrated – on customers, on creditors and on shareholders. In many cases in the Court of Law, I have myself sought to pull aside the curtain: but the majority view is against it. The only machinery so far provided by Parliament is for the Department of Trade to appoint inspectors to hold an inquiry. The inspectors are usually an eminent Queen's Counsel – all Queen's Counsel are by definition 'eminent' – and a distinguished chartered accountant – equally all are 'distinguished'. They have a very unenviable task. They have to investigate all that the directors and managers have done and to report upon it. These inquiries have been known to take years. They involve great expense. And at the end – as often as not – the inspectors are criticised. It is said that they acted unfairly: and that their report should be ignored. The matter is of such importance that we have endeavoured to lay down the principles on which inspectors should act.

2 The Pergamon Press

The issues were raised acutely when there was an inquiry into the affairs of Pergamon Press Ltd. It was held by two good men. Mr. Owen Stable QC – a son of Mr. Justice Stable – and himself of judicial calibre: and Mr. Ronald Leach CBE, (now Sir Ronald Leach, GBE), the senior partner of Peat Marwick. You could not find a better pair anywhere. They had trouble with Mr. Robert Maxwell from the very start. When he came to give evidence, this is what happened (see *Re Pergamon Press Ltd* [1971] Ch 388 at 398):

'A little later the inspectors called on the directors to give evidence. Each of them refused. Typical was the attitude of Mr. Robert Maxwell himself. He came with his solicitor, Mr. Freeman, to the place where the inspectors were meeting. He gave his name and address and said that he was the holder of the Military Cross and a member of Parliament. Then Mr. Stable, a Queen's Counsel, one of the inspectors, asked him this simple question. "When did you first become associated with Pergamon Press Ltd?" to which Mr. Maxwell replied: "Mr. Stable, in view of the submissions made on my behalf by Mr. Freeman, I respectfully refuse to answer any further questions unless I am ordered to do so by the court". This attitude left the inspectors with no alternative but to report the refusal to the court'.

This is how we concluded (at page 401):

'They had promised full co-operation, yet when asked the simple question: "When did you first become associated with Pergamon Press Ltd?" each of them refused to answer. No wonder the inspectors certified their refusal to the court. No wonder the court held their refusal to be unjustified. The judge was merciful to them. He did no more than order them to pay the costs of the application. If they should seek to take again such unwarranted points, they can expect no mercy. They will be treated in like manner as if they had been guilty of contempt of court'.

Afterwards the inspectors proceeded with their inquiry and made an interim report. Mr. Maxwell made complaint about it. He asked for an injunction to restrain the inspectors going on with the inquiry. There was a difference between the two Judges about the legal position. This I sought to solve in this way (see *Maxwell v Department of Trade* [1974] QB 523 at 533):

'In view of this difference between the judges, I will try to state the considerations which are to be borne in mind in respect of an inquiry under the Companies Act 1948. First and foremost: when a matter is referred to an inspector for investigation and report, it is a very special kind of inquiry. It must not be confused with other inquiries which we have had to consider. Remember what it is *not*. It is *not* a trial of anyone, nor anything like it. There is no accused person. There is no prosecutor. There is no charge. It is not like a disciplinary proceeding before a professional body. Nor is it like an application to expel a man from a trade union or a club, or anything of that kind. It is not even like a committee which considers whether there is a prima facie case against a person. It is simply an investigation, without anyone being accused.

'Second: there is no one to present a case to the inspector. There is no "counsel for the commission". The inspector has to do it all himself. He has himself to seek out the relevant documents and to gather the witnesses. He has himself to study the documents, to examine the witnesses and to have their evidence recorded. He has himself to direct the witnesses to the relevant matters. He has himself to cross-examine them to test their accuracy or their veracity. No one else is there to crossexamine them. Even if a witness says things prejudicial to someone else, that other does not hear it and is not there to crossexamine him.

'Third: the investigation is in private. This is necessary because witnesses may say something defamatory of someone else, and it would be quite wrong for it to be published without the party affected being able to challenge it. The only persons present are the inspectors and their staff, the shorthand writer, the witness and his lawyers, if he desires them.

'Fourth: the inspectors have to make their report. They should state their findings on the evidence and their opinions on the matters referred to them. If their report is to be of value, they should make it with courage and frankness, keeping nothing back. The public interest demands it. It may on occasion be necessary for them to condemn or criticise a man. Before doing so, they must act fairly by him. . . .

. . . .

'. . . . It must be remembered that the inspectors are doing a public duty in the public interest. They must do what is fair to the best of their ability. They will, of course, put to a witness the points of substance which occur to them – so as to give him the chance to explain or correct any relevant statement which is prejudicial to him. They may even recall him to do so. But they are not to be criticised because they may on occasion overlook something or other. Even the most skilled advocate, expert in crossexamination, forgets now and again to put this or that point to a witness. And we all excuse him, knowing how difficult it is to remember everything. The inspector is entitled to at least as much consideration as the advocate. To borrow from Shakespeare, he is not to have "all his faults observed, set in a notebook, learn'd, and conn'd by rote", to make a lawyer's holiday. His task is burdensome and thankless enough as it is. It would be intolerable if he were liable to be pilloried afterwards for doing it. No one of standing would ever be found to undertake it. The public interest demands that, so long as he acts honestly and does what is fair to the best of his ability, his report is not to be impugned in the courts of law.

. . . .

'In conclusion, I would say this: I have studied all the points of detail which have been put to us. And I have read the judgment of Wien J upon them. I would like to express my appreciation of it and endorse all that he said. This is nothing more nor less than an attempt by Mr. Maxwell to appeal from the findings of the inspectors to the courts. But Parliament has given no appeal. So Mr. Maxwell has tried to get round it by attacking the conduct of the inspectors themselves. In this he has failed utterly. To my mind the inspectors did their work with conspicuous fairness. They investigated all the matters with the greatest care. They went meticulously into the details of these complicated transactions. They put to Mr. Maxwell all the points which appeared to call for an explanation or an answer. They gave him every opportunity of dealing with them. If there were one or two points which they overlooked, these were as nothing in relation to the wide field which they covered. I regret that, having done their work so well, they should now be harassed by this attack upon them. It has never been done before in all the many inquiries under the Companies Acts. And I hope it will never happen again. . .'.

3 Can the directors stop it?

In the next case the company hit out at an early stage. They tried to stop the inspectors from starting an inquiry at all. They said that the Secretary of State had done wrong in appointing them. It was in *Norwest Holst v Secretary of State for Trade*[1]. This is how we dealt with it:

'It is important to know the background of the legislation. It sometimes happens that public companies are conducted in a way which is beyond the control of the ordinary shareholders. The majority of the shares are in the hands of two or three individuals. These have control of the company's affairs. The other shareholders know little and are told little. They receive the glossy annual reports. Most of them throw them into the wastepaper basket. There is an annual general meeting but few of the shareholders attend. The whole management and control is in the hands of the directors. They are a self-perpetuating oligarchy: and are virtually unaccountable. Seeing that the directors are the guardians of the company, the question is asked: "Quis custodiet ipsos custodes" — Who will guard the guards themselves?
. . . .

   'It is because companies are beyond the reach of ordinary individuals that this legislation has been passed so as to

1. [1978] Ch 201 at 223.

enable the Department of Trade to appoint inspectors to investigate the affairs of a company. . . .

'. . . . There are many cases where an inquiry is held — not as a judicial or quasi-judicial inquiry — but simply as a matter of good administration. In these circumstances there is no need to give preliminary notice of any charge, or anything of that sort. Take the case where a police officer is suspected of misconduct. The practice is to suspend him pending inquiries. He is not given notice of any charge at that stage, nor any opportunity of being heard. The rules of natural justice do not apply unless and until it is decided to take proceedings. Other instances can be given in other fields. For instance, The Stock Exchange may suspend dealings in a company's shares. They go by what they know, without warning the company beforehand.

. . . .

'We know that, when these inquiries are held, those persons who are the subject of them often complain about them. They say that the machinery operates unfairly against them. Such complaints are usually unfounded. They are made so as to delay the inquiry, or to lessen the effect of the report of the inspectors. But, whether well founded or unfounded, it is no reason for abandoning this machinery. It is the only means given to the public by which the conduct of companies can be investigated. Parliament has clearly enacted that there should be power — under the control of the Board of Trade, on behalf of the public at large — for an inquiry to be made into the conduct of the affairs of a company, if there are circumstances which appear to the minister to suggest "fraud, misfeasance or other misconduct". I do not think we should encourage or support any attempt to delay or hold up the inquiry. To my mind the action is without foundation. The judge was quite right to strike it out'.

4 A useful weapon

Parliament has, however, given a weapon which may be useful sometimes to detect fraud. It is something akin to a search warrant. It is given by section 441 of the Companies Act 1948. It enables a judge to make an order for the inspection of a company's books — in cases where it is suspected that there has been an offence in connection with the management of a company's affairs.

It came to our notice when a company contracted to do work on the terms that it should be paid on 'cost plus' terms: that is, it should be paid the amount it had paid to its subcontractor, plus a profit of 20 per cent for itself. Instead of making out this account honestly, they entered into their books a higher sum as 'cost' than they had actually paid the subcontractor. Whilst this fraudulent method was being perpetrated, they took on a new employee in their accounts department. He discovered the fraud. He told the management they ought not to do it. He was dismissed. He told the police. They told the Director of Public Prosecutions. He could do nothing unless he could see the company's books of account — to see what they paid the subcontractor and so forth. If the company were warned beforehand, the evidence might soon disappear. So the Director of Public Prosecutions took advantage of section 441 of the Companies Act 1948. He went to a High Court judge and applied *ex parte* for an order authorising his officers to inspect the books and requiring the Secretary to produce them. The judge felt that the statute should be construed narrowly and refused to make any such order.

The Director of Public Prosecutions wanted to appeal to us. He gave notice and we were all ready to hear it. Then to our surprise we were told the appeal would not be effective. It would only be put into the list 'to be mentioned' and then withdrawn. When it was mentioned, counsel got up and told us the reason. It was because there was a clause in section 441 which said: 'The decision of a judge of the High Court on an application under this Section shall not be appealable'. We exploded at once. We could not allow such a clause to prevent us hearing an appeal — if the judge had gone wrong in his law. That only applied if he had gone wrong on the facts. So we had it put into the list for a full hearing. We had the assistance of the Official Solicitor who instructed counsel. As it was urgent, we heard it on the last day of the summer term. We allowed the appeal and authorised the Director of Public Prosecutions to go ahead. He was empowered to inspect the books and require the Secretary to produce them. The case is entitled *Re a Company*[1].

1. (1979) 123 Sol Jo 584, CA.

4 Into the conduct of gaming clubs

In most inquiries, the rules of natural justice apply. If the conduct of a person is under investigation he is entitled to know what is said against him so that he can answer it. But there are exceptions: especially where information is given by 'informers'. Their names may have to be kept secret — else the source of information would dry up. Even the information itself may have to be limited. It is a nice question which came up for discussion in the case of *R v Gaming Board*[1].

Crockford's is one of the most famous gaming clubs in London. It has premises of distinction at 16 Carlton House Terrace. They play there the familiar games: chemin-de-fer, baccarat, roulette, blackjack and craps. (Some years after this case I went there myself — not to play any game whatever: but to open a display of Magna Carta: and to have a good dinner). By the Gaming Act 1968 all these gaming clubs had to have a licence and for this purpose they had to apply to the Gaming Board for a 'certificate of consent'. Crockford's duly applied, but the Gaming Board refused it. They said that those who ran the club were associated 'with certain persons of unacceptable background and reputation'.

The Board refused to disclose some confidential information which they had. Thereupon Crockford's instructed that redoubtable advocate, Mr. Quintin Hogg QC (as he then was). The Board instructed a first-class opponent, Mr. Raymond Kidwell QC. We had on that occasion Lord Wilberforce with

1. [1970] 2 WLR 1009.

us. On very rare occasions if the House can spare us a Law Lord, he comes to help us. It was an infinite advantage to have Lord Wilberforce — the best judicial mind of the day. There were several points in the case but on this matter of disclosure of the source of information, this is what I said (at page 1017):

'I do not think they need tell the applicant the source of their information, if that would put their informant in peril or otherwise be contrary to the public interest. Even in a criminal trial, a witness cannot be asked who is his informer. The reason was well given by Lord Eyre CJ in *Hardy's* case [*R v Hardy*] 24 State Trials 199, 808: ".... there is a rule which has universally obtained on account of its importance to the public for the detection of crimes, that those persons who are the channel by means of which that detection is made, should not be unnecessarily disclosed".

'And Buller J added, at p.818: ".... if you call for the name of the informer in such cases, no man will make a discovery, and public justice will be defeated" .... That reasoning applies with equal force to the inquiries made by the Gaming Board. That board was set up by Parliament to cope with disreputable gaming clubs and to bring them under control. By bitter experience it was learned that these clubs had a close connection with organised crime, often violent crime, with protection rackets and with strong-arm methods. If the Gaming Board were bound to disclose their sources of information, no one would "tell" on those clubs, for fear of reprisals. Likewise with the details of the information. If the board were bound to disclose every detail, that might itself give the informer away and put him in peril. But, without disclosing every detail, I should have thought that the board ought in every case to be able to give to the applicant sufficient indication of the objections raised against him such as to enable him to answer them. That is only fair. And the board must at all costs be fair. If they are not, these courts will not hesitate to interfere.

'Accepting that the board ought to do all this when they come to give their decision, the question arises, are they bound to give their reasons? I think not. Magistrates are not bound to give reasons for their decisions: see *R v Northumberland Compensation Appeal Tribunal, ex parte Shaw*[1]. Nor should the Gaming Board be bound. After all, the only thing that they have to give is their *opinion* as to the capability and diligence of the applicant. If they were asked by the applicant to give their reasons, they could answer quite sufficiently: "In our opinion, you are not likely to be capable of or diligent in the respects required of you". Their opinion would be an end of the matter.

'Tested by those rules, applying them to this case, I think that the Gaming Board acted with complete fairness. . .'.

That ruling came up for consideration by the House of Lords two years later. Henry Rogers wanted to manage bingo halls. He applied to the Gaming Board for consent. They refused. It appears that they had asked the Chief Constable of Sussex for a report about Rogers. The Chief Constable had given the Gaming Board information which was highly defamatory of Rogers. The Board had this report before them but did not show it to Rogers. Afterwards, someone in some way — very devious, no doubt — abstracted it from the file and gave a copy of it to Rogers. Rogers sought to take proceedings for libel. He failed. The case went as far as the House of Lords. It is *R v Lewes JJ*[2] in which Lord Reid approved our decision, saying:

'Natural justice requires that the board should act in good faith and that they should, as far as possible, tell him the gist of any grounds on which they propose to refuse his application so that he may show it to be unfounded in fact. But the board must be trusted to do that: we have been referred to their practice in the matter and I see nothing wrong with it'.

1. [1952] 1 KB 338 at 352.
2. [1973] AC 388 at 402.

5 Into the conduct of aliens

Now there is one type of inquiry in which natural justice is excluded. It is when it is necessary in the interests of national security. There is some information which is so secret that it cannot be disclosed — except to a very few. This country, like all others, has its own intelligence service. It has its own spies or agents, just as others have. Their very lives may be endangered if there is the slightest hint of what they are doing. In one case (of which the public know nothing) many of our agents disappeared. They were lost beyond trace. They were 'eliminated' by a foreign power. The information is known to the Security Service but to no one outside.

It is information of this kind which was hinted at — no more than hinted at — in the case of Mark Hosenball, *R v Home Secretary, ex parte Hosenball*[1]. We did not compel disclosure of it — and for it we have been criticised in many quarters. So I would like to explain it.

Mark Hosenball was an American journalist. He came here when he was only 18 and took part in investigative journalism. He had permission from the Home Office to be here. His permit had four weeks to go when (page 777):

'. . . he received a letter from the Home Office. It told him that he could no longer stay because the Secretary of State had decided to deport him. The reason was because it was in the interests of national security. I will read the statement which was enclosed with the letter. . . .

'That statement is couched in official language: but translated into plain English it means that the Secretary of

1. [1977] 1 WLR 766.

State believes that Mr. Hosenball is a danger to this country. So much so that his presence here is unwelcome and he can no longer be permitted to stay. This belief is founded on confidential information which has been placed before the Home Secretary. It is to the effect that Mr. Hosenball is one of a group of people who are trying to obtain information of a very sensitive character about our security arrangements. Their intention is to publish it, or some of it, in a way which will imperil the lives of the men in our secret service. The crucial charge against him is that he has "information prejudicial to the safety of the servants of the Crown" and is proposing to publish it. If that charge be true, he should certainly be deported. We cannot allow our men's lives to be endangered by foreigners.

. . . .

'Now I would like to say at once that if this were a case in which the ordinary rules of natural justice were to be observed, some criticism could be directed upon it. For one thing the Home Secretary himself, and I expect the advisory panel also, had a good deal of confidential information before them of which Mr. Hosenball knew nothing and was told nothing: and which he had no opportunity of correcting or contradicting, or of testing by crossexamination. In addition, he was not given sufficient information of the charges against him so as to be able effectively to deal with them or answer them. All this could be urged as a ground for upsetting any ordinary decision of a court of law or of any tribunal, statutory or domestic. . . .

'But this is no ordinary case. It is a case in which national security is involved: and our history shows that, when the state itself is endangered, our cherished freedoms may have to take second place. Even natural justice itself may suffer a set-back. Time after time Parliament has so enacted and the courts have loyally followed. In the first world war in *R v Halliday*[1] Lord Finlay LC said: "The danger of espionage and of damage by secret agents . . . . had to be guarded

1. [1917] AC 260 at 270.

against". In the second world war in *Liversidge v Sir John Anderson*[1] Lord Maugham said:

". . . . there may be certain persons against whom no offence is proved nor any charge formulated, but as regards whom it may be expedient to authorise the Secretary of State to make an order for detention".

'That was said in time of war. But times of peace hold their dangers too. Spies, subverters and saboteurs may be mingling amongst us, putting on a most innocent exterior. They may be endangering the lives of the men in our secret service, as Mr. Hosenball is said to do.

'If they are British subjects, we must deal with them here. If they are foreigners, they can be deported. The rules of natural justice have to be modified in regard to foreigners here who prove themselves unwelcome and ought to be deported.

. . . .

'The information supplied to the Home Secretary by the Security Service is, and must be, highly confidential. The public interest in the security of the realm is so great that the sources of the information must not be disclosed — nor should the nature of the information itself be disclosed — if there is any risk that it would lead to the sources being discovered. The reason is because, in this very secretive field, our enemies might try to eliminate the sources of information. So the sources must not be disclosed. Not even to the House of Commons. Nor to any tribunal or court of inquiry or body of advisers, statutory or non-statutory. Save to the extent that the Home Secretary thinks safe. Great as is the public interest in the freedom of the individual and the doing of justice to him, nevertheless in the last resort it must take second place to the security of the country itself. So much so that arrests have not been made, nor proceedings instituted, for fear that it may give away information which must be kept secret. This is in keeping with all our recent cases about confidential information. When the public interest requires

---

1. [1942] AC 206 at 219.

that information be kept confidential, it may outweigh even the public interest in the administration of justice. . . .

. . . .

'There is a conflict here between the interests of national security on the one hand and the freedom of the individual on the other. The balance between these two is not for a court of law. It is for the Home Secretary. He is the person entrusted by Parliament with the task. In some parts of the world national security has on occasions been used as an excuse for all sorts of infringements of individual liberty. But not in England. Both during the wars and after them, successive ministers have discharged their duties to the complete satisfaction of the people at large. They have set up advisory committees to help them, usually with a chairman who has done everything he can to ensure that justice is done. They have never interfered with the liberty or the freedom of movement of any individual except where it is absolutely necessary for the safety of the state. In this case we are assured that the Home Secretary himself gave it his personal consideration, and I have no reason whatever to doubt the care with which he considered the whole matter. He is answerable to Parliament as to the way in which he did it and not to the courts here'.

6 Into the delays of lawyers

1 Into the Courts of Law

Ever since lawyers have been going, the layman has complained of their delays: and for just so long, the lawyers have been making excuses. The most common excuse is their busyness. You will remember that some 600 years ago Chaucer said of the Sergeant of the Lawe:

'No-wher so bisy a man as he ther nas,
   And yet he semed bisier than he was'.

It is, I know, a common ploy among barristers to 'seme bisier' than they are. If you are busy, you are successful: if you are not busy, you are a failure. So it is important to 'seme bisy'. I well remember when I was young at the bar — and expecting a client — I would set out on my table the briefs and cases for opinion, all tied up in red tape, so as to seem busy. But most of them would be 'dead'. They had been finished and done with long before. It was only after ten years or so that my table would be crowded out with 'live' instructions piling one on another.

The real reason for the delays of lawyers is not slackness or dilatoriness. They are as a class the most hardworking of all professional men. It often lies in their choice of priorities. Each case is important and must be dealt with. Each letter must be answered the same day or at any rate the next. A sudden call puts something else out of mind. Sometimes it is that he is a slow worker. More often that he is too meticulous. Sometimes it is that he does not know

89

enough, and has to look it all up. Sometimes that he is short of staff or someone falls ill. All these are excuses which may avail him before the Almighty. But none of them avail him before the individual client. Nor before us. The courts expect each client's case to be dealt with expeditiously. At any rate they have so expected since our great case of *Allen v McAlpine*[1]. I describe it as a 'great case' because we reserved it over the Christmas vacation: and at the time Lord Justice Diplock remarked to me that it was the most important we had done.

Let me explain first that, in a civil case, the pace is set by the plaintiff who is making the claim. It is he who has to issue the writ and to serve it. It is he who has to put in the statement of claim and to serve it. It is he who can call upon the defendant to put in a defence or else suffer the consequences. If the plaintiff himself takes a long time over the things he has to do, the case may drag on indefinitely. And so it used to be before *Allen v McAlpine*. The Rules laid down a timetable with which the plaintiff was supposed to comply: but he never suffered for his non-compliance. He always got an extension of time for the asking. I cannot do better than set out the opening pages of our judgment[2]:

'In these three cases the law's delays have been intolerable. They have lasted so long as to turn justice sour. I will give details later, but in outline they stand thus. In the first case a widow lost her husband nearly *nine* years ago. He was killed at his work. She had a good claim to compensation from his employers for herself and her two small children. Her case has not yet been set down for trial. In the second case, a nurse complained that she strained her back over *nine* years ago whilst lifting a patient. It meant a year off work. If her story is true, she was entitled to compensation from the hospital authorities. They have not even yet put in a defence to the claim. In the third case, a man of business bought shares nearly *fourteen* years ago for £20,000. He brought

1. [1968] 2 QB 229, [1968] 2 WLR 366.
2. [1968] 2 WLR 366 at 369—371.

an action complaining that he was deceived in the deal, and that his company was let down by the solicitors. The man who sold the shares has since died. His estate cannot be administered whilst this suit is hanging over it. His widow cannot receive the money he bequeathed to her. Yet the suit has not yet been entered for trial.

'In none of the three cases has the party himself been at fault. The widow, the nurse and the man of business, each one of them wanted to get on. The fault, I regret to say, has been with the legal advisers. It is not that they wilfully neglected the cases. But they have put them on one side, sometimes for months, and even for years, because of the pressure of other work or of other claims on their time. Hence these ills. And these are not the only examples. A few months ago we had a couple of cases of like sort. One was on 9 March 1967, *Reggentin v Beecholme Bakeries Ltd*[1]. The other was on 17 March 1967, *Fitzpatrick v Batger & Co Ltd*[2]. We said[3]: "Delay in these cases is much to be deplored. It is the duty of the plaintiff's advisers to get on with the case. Every year that passes prejudices the fair trial". We struck out those cases for want of prosecution. This meant that the injured plaintiffs could not recover their compensation from the defendants. But they could recover it from their own negligent solicitors. These cases have brought home to lawyers that they must get on. A note in the Supreme Court Practice (1967) 2nd supp., p.4, para. 25/1/3, says that: "These emphatic decisions of the Court of Appeal, which lay down a more stringent practice than was formerly followed, have injected a new element of expedition in the conduct and preparation of cases before trial, especially in relation to 'accident' cases. Plaintiffs' solicitors who do not 'get on' with their cases will be at risk of having the plaintiff's action dismissed for want of prosecution and themselves rendered liable for negligence to the plaintiff as their own former client".

1. (1967) 111 Sol Jo 216.
2. [1967] 2 All ER 657, [1967] 1 WLR 706, CA.
3. (1967) 111 Sol Jo 216, CA.

'Following those decisions, several other cases have been struck out for delay. These three are among them. The plaintiffs appeal to this court. I say "the plaintiffs" appeal, but we cannot shut our eyes to the fact that the plaintiffs' solicitors and their insurers are very much concerned in the appeals lest they be held liable for negligence. The Law Society too are concerned, for counsel appeared for them and asked to be heard. We permitted him as amicus curiae to address us on the issues of public policy involved.

'It was urged that we ought not to strike out a man's action without trial because it meant depriving him of his right to come to the Queen's Courts. Magna Carta was invoked against us as if we were in some way breaking its provisions. To this there is a short answer. The delay of justice is a denial of justice. Magna Carta will have none of it. "To no one will we deny or delay right or justice"[1].

'All through the years men have protested at the law's delay and counted it as a grievous wrong, hard to bear. Shakespeare ranks it among the whips and scorns of time[2]. Dickens tells how it exhausts finances, patience, courage, hope[3]. To put right this wrong, we will in this court do all in our power to enforce expedition: and, if need be, we will strike out actions when there has been excessive delay. This is a stern measure. But it is within the inherent jurisdiction of the court. And the Rules of Court expressly permit it. It is the only effective sanction they contain. If a plaintiff fails within the specified time to deliver a statement of claim, or to take out a summons for directions, or to set down the action for trial, the defendant can apply for the action to be dismissed, see R.S.C. (Rev. 1965), Ord. 19, r. 1; Ord. 25, r. 1; Ord. 34, r. 2. It was argued before us that the court should never, on the first application, dismiss the action. Even if there was long delay, the court should always give the dilatory solicitor one more chance. The order should be that the action should be dismissed "unless" he takes the

1. Magna Carta, ch. 40.
2. *Hamlet*, Act III, sc. 1.
3. *Bleak House*, ch. 1.

next step within a stated time. Such has been the practice, it was said, for a great many years. It was confirmed by Sir George Jessel MR in *Eaton v Storer*[1] and it should not be changed without prior notice. I cannot accept this suggestion. If there were such a practice, there would be no sanction whatever against delay. The plaintiff's solicitor could put a case on one side as long as he pleased without fear of the consequences.

'If you read *Eaton v Storer*[2] carefully, you will see that the practice described by Sir George Jessel applies only to moderate delays of two or three months. It does not apply when "there is some special circumstance such as excessive delay"[3]. The principle upon which we go is clear: When the delay is prolonged and inexcusable, and is such as to do grave injustice to one side or the other or to both, the court may in its discretion dismiss the action straightaway, leaving the plaintiff to his remedy against his own solicitor who has brought him to this plight. Whenever a solicitor, by his inexcusable delay, deprives a client of his cause of action, the client can claim damages against him; as, for instance, when a solicitor does not issue a writ in time, or serve it in time, or does not renew it properly. We have seen, I regret to say, several such cases lately. Not a few are legally aided. In all of them the solicitors have, I believe, been quick to compensate the suffering client; or at least their insurers have. So the wrong done by the delay has been remedied as much as can be. I hope this will always be done'.

But it was not my judgment which carried the day. It was perhaps too general. It was the judgments of Lord Justice Diplock and Lord Justice Salmon. They spelt it out more precisely. In order to dismiss an action for want of prosecution there must have been inordinate and inexcusable delay which was such as to cause serious prejudice to the defendant. We did not realise it at the time but this formulation gave rise to great difficulties in regard to the Statutes of Limitation.

1. (1882) 22 Ch D 91 at 92.
2. (1882) 22 Ch D 91.
3. Ibid. at 92.

In cases of personal injury the plaintiff had to issue his writ within three years of the accident and serve it within a further one year. If the plaintiff took the whole of that time — four years — before he served his writ, the defendant would have suffered an immense prejudice by that delay. Now this is the point which divided the Court of Appeal:

In one division of the Court, presided over by Russell LJ, it was said that the plaintiff had a *right* to take those four years: and that delay and prejudice in that time did not matter much. That was in *Parker v Hann*[1]. But in the division presided over by me, we rejected that view. In *Sweeney v Sir Robert McAlpine & Sons*[2], I said:

'. . . . The plaintiff has no such right. He is not entitled to delay at all. It is his duty to make his claim and bring his proceedings with all expedition at all stages. If he is guilty of inordinate and inexcusable delay — finishing up with a failure to observe the Rules of Court as to time — he is liable to have his action dismissed for want of prosecution, if the total delay is such as seriously to prejudice the defendants. . .'.

That view became accepted generally. It was applied by the Court of Appeal in *Birkett v James*[3] but afterwards, I regret to say, it was reversed by the House of Lords. The story is so illuminating that I will tell it. The plaintiff, Mr. Birkett, alleged that the defendant, Mr. James, agreed *orally* in November 1969 to pay him £1,000,000 on 1 April 1970. That very allegation makes it look a doubtful case. Nothing in writing to support an agreement for £1,000,000! The plaintiff did not show much confidence in it himself. He did nothing for over two years. Then in July 1972 the plaintiff got legal aid and issued a writ claiming the £1,000,000. But he or his then solicitor delayed for many, many months to pursue the claim. So much so that in July 1975 the defendant issued a summons to dismiss it for want

1. [1972] 1 WLR 1583.
2. [1974] 1 WLR 200 at 205.
3. [1978] AC 297 at 301.

of prosecution. The Judge did dismiss it. So did the Court of Appeal. They held that the delay was altogether inordinate and inexcusable and that the defendant was seriously prejudiced by it. They refused leave to appeal. Now I pause here to say that, in cases of this kind, being what we call interlocutory matters, the view of the Court of Appeal is usually regarded as final. But in this case the plaintiff, with the help of legal aid, went to the House of Lords, got leave to appeal, did appeal, and succeeded in his appeal. The House were much influenced by the fact that, in cases of breach of contract, the period of limitation is six years. So that, although more than five years had elapsed since 1 April 1970, the plaintiff could issue another writ. In those circumstances the House allowed the stale action to continue. They made the defendant pay all the costs. The action went for trial.

The rest of the tale is not told in the Law Reports. At the trial the plaintiff's claim was held to be hopeless. I believe that it was dismissed without even calling upon the defendant. It shows that much injustice can be done when the House grants leave to appeal. It meant that the defendant had to pay the very great expense of appeal to the Lords without getting a penny back from the plaintiff who had sued him without any real foundation for his claim.

Since that time the Court of Appeal has done all it can to mitigate the effect of *Birkett v James*. Notably in *Biss v Lambeth Health Authority*[1] and *Mahon v Concrete (Southern) Ltd*[2]. But its unfortunate influence was most marked in *Tolley v Morris*[3]. There, in May 1964 a little girl of 2½ was injured in an accident by a motorcar. Three years later a writ was issued on her behalf by her father as her next friend. It was served within another year. That was in March 1968. But then nothing more was done for nine years – until July 1977. That is 13 years after the accident. By that time the witnesses had disappeared – all memory had gone – the police record

1. [1978] 1 WLR 382.
2. (1979) 6 July (not yet reported).
3. [1979] 1 WLR 592.

files had been destroyed — a fair trial was impossible. It was clearly a case where it would have been dismissed for want of prosecution — but for *Birkett v James*. Yet because the little girl was still under 18 — and so the period of limitation had not expired — the action was allowed to continue. But it was only by a majority of 3 to 2 in the House of Lords. Lord Wilberforce and Lord Dilhorne dissented. Many would have thought that their view should have prevailed.

I have often thought that the argument — that the plaintiff can issue another writ — is fallacious. If the first action should be dismissed, then let it be dismissed. The plaintiff may not have the hardihood to start another: nor should he get legal aid for it. Even if he should start a second action, he ought to pay the defendant all the costs incurred in the first.

Since the Limitation Act 1975, the period of three years is not an absolute bar. The Court has a discretion to extend the time but still in exercising its discretion, the delay of the plaintiff or his solicitors is the most important consideration in deciding whether or not the action should be allowed to continue. It may be that the ruling in *Birkett v James* can be discarded and the principles of the Court of Appeal applied in their full force.

2 Can anything be done about arbitration?

Thus far I have spoken about delays in litigation before the Courts. If a plaintiff is guilty of inordinate and inexcusable delay, his action can be dismissed for want of prosecution. But many disputes are referred to arbitration. In commerce and industry today, most contracts of any magnitude contain provisions for arbitration. Disputes about ships or building works all go to arbitration. Huge sums are in issue. Some awarded. Some rejected.

Suppose now that a claimant in an arbitration is guilty of inordinate and inexcusable delay — and that the delay is so serious that a fair hearing is impossible — has the other side any remedy? Until recently it was thought that there was none. In *Crawford v Prowting Ltd*[1] Bridge J held that an arbitrator had no power to dismiss a claim for want of prosecution. An arbitrator was bound to allow the claimant — no matter how long his delay — more time to get on with his case. The Commercial Court Committee took the same view. They thought that it was a great deficiency that there was no sanction against delay in arbitrations. One or other side could drag its feet and put off the day of judgment — or rather of the award — indefinitely. Mr. Justice Donaldson was the Chairman of that Committee. (He was at one time Chairman of the Industrial Relations Court and did it splendidly — though much abused in some quarters.) Yet it was he who recently held there was a remedy available in respect of delay in arbitration. It was in two cases just reported in *Bremer Vulkan v South India Shipping*[2]. He declined to follow the previous decision of Bridge J. He held that arbitrators had the same power as a Court to dismiss for want of prosecution: and further that where the claimant had been guilty of inordinate and inexcusable delay, the other side could apply to the Court for an injunction: and that the Court could order the claimant to desist from proceeding further with the arbitration. In the two cases he granted injunctions stopping the arbitrations. That was in April 1979. His decision was followed a few weeks later by Lloyd J in *The Splendid Sun*[3].

We must reserve our views on the correctness of these decisions: because they are under appeal to the Court of Appeal. They are, as Donaldson J said, of fundamental importance to English arbitration. To some extent the Legislature has already gone along the same road as Donaldson J. By Section 5 of the Arbitration Act 1979 an arbitrator may in future have like power as a Court to dismiss for want of prosecution. So progress is being made.

1. [1973] QB 1.
2. [1979] 3 WLR 471.
3. (1979) 4 May (not yet reported).

Part three

Arrest and search

Introduction

Long have I associated myself with human rights. My Hamlyn Lectures in 1949 were concerned with personal freedom, freedom of speech and the rest. But on looking back over the cases of the intervening 30 years, I find that I have been concerned – not so much with freedom – as with keeping the balance between freedom and security. As I said in 1949 of personal freedom:

'It must be matched, of course, with social security, by which I mean, the peace and good order of the community in which we live. The freedom of the just man is worth little to him if he can be preyed upon by the murderer or the thief. Every society must have means to protect itself from marauders. It must have powers to arrest, to search and to imprison those who break its laws. So long as those powers are properly exercised, they are the safeguards of freedom. But powers may be abused, and if those powers are abused, there is no tyranny like them'.

1 Making an arrest

1 The role of the police

In safeguarding our freedoms, the police play a vital role. Society for its defence needs a well-led, well-trained and well-disciplined force of police whom it can trust: and enough of them to be able to prevent crime before it happens, or if it does happen, to detect it and bring the accused to justice.

The police, of course, must act properly. They must obey the rules of right conduct. They must not extort confessions by threats or promises. They must not search a man's house without authority. They must not use more force than the occasion warrants. But, so long as they act honourably and properly, all honest citizens should support them to the uttermost. There is nothing more detrimental to the rule of law than for the kidnapper to extract his ransom and get clear; for the mugger to smash up old ladies and go free; or for the company director to defraud the shareholders and get away with it.

One of the most disturbing features of life in our time is the way wrongdoers seek to discredit the guardians of the peace. If hooligans demonstrate in the street, lie down in the highway and obstruct it, whenever they are removed there is the cat-call, 'Police brutality'. If a man makes a statement to the police and it is given in evidence in the Court, as often as not he will turn round and say it was extracted by threats, or was made up, or that he was framed.

The time has come when it is the duty of every responsible citizen to support the police and to recognise that they are the front line of defence against violence and intimidation:

102

and then it is the duty of the courts to uphold the powers of arrest — and of search and seizure — when they are properly exercised.

So I make no apology if in these pages, I recount the principles which go towards the safeguarding of freedom.

2 'Come along with me'

When a police constable says to a man, 'Come along with me. I am taking you to the station', that is an arrest. No matter if the man goes quietly or resists with all his strength, it is an arrest. If it is a lawful arrest, the man cannot complain. If it is unlawful, the man can bring an action for false imprisonment and get damages. So it is very important for the constable to know what his powers are. Everyone is entitled, and indeed it is his duty, to intervene when there is a breach of the peace being committed in his presence or when any other arrestable offence is actually being committed. But in all other cases his better course is to call the police. Now our law about arrest is very complicated. I have been to the Staff College for the Police at Bramshill in Hampshire: and I have talked to them. I am impressed by their high standards. But one of the most difficult and important things for a constable to know is when he is empowered to make an arrest: and what he can then do. The Commandant told me that they always tell their officers about *Dallison v Caffery*[1].

3 Identification by a photograph

It was a typical story. It is repeated a hundred times a year: but as it has so many lessons I will repeat it here. A typist was working in a solicitor's office in Dunstable. She went to the bank, collected the money and put £173 in the safe. She shut the door of the safe but did not lock it. She was just leaving for lunch when she saw a man on the landing. She said to him, 'Can I help you?' He turned round and

1. [1965] 1 QB 348.

103

faced her. 'No, I have got the wrong office'. She went upstairs for a few moments. As she came down, she heard a bang and footsteps running down the stairs. The £173 was missing. She called the police. Detective Constable Caffery was in charge. She gave them a description of the man. They took her to the CID office. They showed her some photographs. She picked out the photograph of a criminal well known to the police. It was Dallison. She said, 'That's the man'.

The police went to London. They saw Dallison. He said he was working at another place that day. They did not accept his alibi. They arrested Dallison. They took him to his home. They took him to the place where he said he had been working that day. They searched his house and found nothing. They took him back to Dunstable.

Before taking him back, however, they went to see some very respectable people, Mr. and Mrs. Stamp and Mrs. Lansman. Their evidence tended to support his alibi. An identification parade was held. There were 11 men of somewhat similar appearance to Dallison. The typist went up and down and looked at each man closely. She asked each man to say, 'No, I have got the wrong office'. She said, 'There is only one man who I think it is'. She pointed to Dallison and went up and touched him.

Dallison was taken before the magistrates. The typist was called and the police officer. But not the three people who supported his alibi.

At Quarter Sessions, counsel for the prosecution offered no evidence so Dallison was acquitted. He brought an action for false imprisonment and malicious prosecution. Mr. Jukes QC — very able and persuasive — represented Dallison. The arrest itself was clearly lawful. The typist had picked out Dallison from the photographs: and that was reasonable cause for thinking it was he who committed the offence. But a serious question was raised about their taking him all round London. In giving judgment, I spoke of the law of arrest, using the word 'felony'. At common law all the more serious offences were 'felonies'. The less serious were 'misdemeanours'. That distinction has been abolished now by the

Criminal Law Act 1967. It has been replaced by a newly invented word 'arrestable offence' which again means the more serious offences: but you have to look up the books to find out precisely what they are. Suffice it to say that the judgment I gave there is still apposite: but for 'felony' you should read 'arrestable offence'. This is what I said[1]:

'Mr. Jukes next said that, even if the arrest was justifiable, nevertheless it was not lawful for Detective Constable Caffery to take Dallison to 40 Millfields Road and not to take him straight back to the police station at Dunstable. This raises an interesting point as to the power of the police in regard to a man whom they have in custody. Mr. Jukes says that a constable has no more power than a private person. I cannot agree with this. So far as *arrest* is concerned, a constable has long had more power than a private person. If a constable makes an arrest without a warrant, he can justify it on the ground that he had reasonable cause for suspecting that the accused had committed a felony. He does not have to go further (as a private person has to do) and prove that a felony has in fact been committed. So far as *custody* is concerned, a constable also has extra powers. If a *private person* arrests a man on suspicion of having committed a felony, he cannot take the man round the town seeking evidence against him: . . . The private person must, as soon as he reasonably can, hand the man over to a constable or take him to the police station or take him before a magistrate; but so long as he does so within a reasonable time, he is not to be criticised because he holds the man for a while to consider the position: . . . A *constable,* however, has a greater power. When a constable has taken into custody a person reasonably suspected of felony, he can do what is reasonable to investigate the matter, and to see whether the suspicions are supported or not by further evidence. He can, for instance, take the suspected person to his house to see whether any of the stolen property is there; else it may be removed and valuable evidence lost. He can take the suspected person to

1. [1965] 1 QB 348 at 366.

the place where he says he was working, for there he may find persons to confirm or refute his alibi. The constable can put him up on an identification parade to see if he is picked out by the witnesses. So long as such measures are taken reasonably, they are an important adjunct to the administration of justice. By which I mean, of course, justice not only to the man himself but also to the community at large. The measures must, however, be reasonable. In *Wright v Court*[1] a constable held a man for three days without taking him before a magistrate. The constable pleaded that he did so in order to enable the private prosecutor to collect his evidence. That was plainly unreasonable and the constable's plea was overruled. In this case it is plain to me that the measures taken were reasonable. Indeed, Dallison himself willingly co-operated in all that was done. He cannot complain of it as a false imprisonment. . .'.

4 Should the prosecution tell?

Then there was an interesting question about the three witnesses who were not called before the magistrates. Ought they to have been? On this, I said[2]:

'Next, Mr. Jukes pointed out that, at the committal proceedings, the evidence of Mr. and Mrs. Stamp and Mrs. Lansman was not made available to the magistrates. I do not see that this should be taken against Caffery. He did not conceal these statements. He put them before his superior officers and also before the solicitor for the prosecution. It was not his fault that the solicitor did not think it necessary to put them before the magistrates. Nor do I think the solicitor need have done. The duty of a prosecuting counsel or solicitor, as I have always understood it, is this: if he knows of a credible witness who can speak to material facts which tend to show the prisoner to be innocent, he must either call that witness himself or make his statement available to the defence. It would be highly reprehensible to conceal from the court the

1. (1825) 4 B & C 596.
2. [1965] 1 QB 348 at 368.

evidence which such a witness can give. If the prosecuting counsel or solicitor knows, not of a credible witness, but a witness whom he does not accept as credible, he should tell the defence about him so that they can call him if they wish. Here the solicitor, immediately after the court proceedings, gave the solicitor for the defence the statement of Mr. and Mrs. Stamp; and thereby he did his duty'.

Following this, very recently a conviction was quashed because the police had not told the defendant of witnesses who would assist him[1].

5 Unfit to drive

Such was the power of arrest at common law. But there are many Statutes which now give a power of arrest: and then it is a question of interpreting the Statutes, such as the Road Traffic Acts which give a police constable power to arrest without warrant a man who is unfit to drive a motor vehicle through drink or drugs. This power came up for consideration in *Wiltshire v Barrett*[2]. Two constables saw Mr. Wiltshire driving a car. He was going too fast. They signalled him to stop. He stopped. They asked him his name and address. He said nothing. They asked him to get out of the car. He clung to the steering wheel and said, 'I am not moving'. He was staring ahead with a glassy look in his eyes. They told him they were arresting him for driving while under the influence of drink. They radioed for assistance. Two other police officers came. They got him out of the car and took him to the police station. The doctor found that he had a number of bruises and abrasions and he was of opinion that he was not unfit to drive through drink. Thereupon the police released him without making any charge against him. He brought an action for damages. It took six days. The judge directed the jury that the arrest was unlawful. They awarded

1. *R v Leyland JJ, ex parte Hawthorn* [1979] QB 283.
2. [1966] 1 QB 312.

Mr. Wiltshire £589 damages. The Court of Appeal reversed the decision. I said (page 321):

'The first point: Mr. Fay submitted that this section only empowered a constable to arrest a person who was actually committing an offence under the section: and accordingly the constable was only justified if he could prove that the person was *in fact guilty.* Whereas Mr. Stock submitted that a constable was entitled to arrest any person who was *apparently* committing an offence; and accordingly the constable was justified so long as it *appeared to him* that the man was unfit through drink, even though the man should afterwards be found to be not guilty.

'. . . . This statute is concerned with the safety of all of Her Majesty's subjects who use the roads in this country. It is of the first importance that any person who is unfit to drive through drink should not be allowed to drive on the road, and that the police should have power to stop him from driving any further. The most effective way to do it is by arresting him then and there. The police have to act at once, on the facts *as they appear* on the spot: and they should be justified by the facts as they appear to them at the time and not on any ex post facto analysis of the situation. Their conduct should not be condemned as unlawful simply because a jury afterwards acquit the driver. We all know how merciful some juries are to drivers who have been drinking. As often as not they acquit them. The jurors are inclined to say to themselves: "There but for the grace of God go I". If every motorist who is acquitted is to have an unanswerable claim for damages against the police, I should think that the police would soon give up trying to arrest anyone; and that would be very bad for us all. The police must be entitled to act on the facts as they appear to them at the time'.

The second point was also interesting and is worth recording (page 323):

'The second point: Mr. Fay submitted that an arrest without warrant was only lawful if it was carried through to its conclusion. It could be concluded, he said, either by bringing the man before a magistrate or by his being granted bail at the police station. If he was released before either of these things happened, as in this case, then the arrest was rendered unlawful from the beginning. It became a trespass ab initio. The judge accepted this submission and acted on it. He ruled that, as the plaintiff had been released without being bailed, the arrest was unlawful from the beginning and that the only question for the jury was the amount of damages.

'See what this decision means. Even though the police constable was quite justified in arresting the man and bringing him to the police station, nevertheless the conduct of the officer in charge at the station, in afterwards releasing the man, rendered the conduct of the police constable unlawful from the beginning. Such a proposition is contrary to the general rule that an act which is lawful at the time is not to be rendered unlawful afterwards by the doctrine of relation back . . . and it is decisively negatived by two cases which were cited to us by Mr. Stock.

. . . .

'Since that time it has been settled law that, if after arrest a man is found on inquiry to be innocent, or at any rate that there is no sufficient case for detaining him, he should at once be set free. There is no obligation to take him to the magistrate . . .'.

2 Making a search

Introduction

It is one of the incidents of a power of arrest that if police officers lawfully arrest a man for a felony (now an 'arrestable offence') they can go to his house: and search for and seize any goods which they reasonably believe to be material evidence in relation to the crime for which they arrested him. For instance, whenever a man is arrested for stealing, it is everyday practice to go to his house and see whether the stolen goods are there.

But when they have not arrested a man, and seek to enter his house or anyone else's house – so as to find evidence against him or anyone else – they have to rely *either* on the common law *or* they must get a search warrant authorising them to do so. Each of these situations has been the subject of leading cases in recent years.

1 Passports withheld

Until 1970 we had not had to consider the common law position. But then it arose in a remarkable case, *Ghani v Jones*[1]. There was a Pakistani household living in Oxford. The wife disappeared. The husband went back to Pakistan. The police thought that he had murdered her. His father and mother and sister remained in the house. The police went to the house. They searched it and took the passports of the three of them. They continued their inquiries, still believing – on reasonable grounds – that the husband had murdered

1. [1970] 1 QB 693.

110

his wife. The three in the house then asked for their passports back. They said they wanted to go back to Pakistan for a holiday. The police refused to give them up. We made an order for their release. I tried to set out the law — so as to be a guide for the future. I said[1]:

'So we have a case where the police officers, in investigating a murder, have seized property without a warrant and without making an arrest and have retained it without the consent of the party from whom they took it. Their justification is that they believe it to be of "evidential value" on a prosecution for murder. Is this a sufficient justification in law?
. . . .
'What is the principle underlying these instances? We have to consider, on the one hand, the freedom of the individual. His privacy and his possessions are not to be invaded except for the most compelling reasons. On the other hand, we have to consider the interest of society at large in finding out wrongdoers and repressing crime. Honest citizens should help the police and not hinder them in their efforts to track down criminals. Balancing these interests, I should have thought that, in order to justify the taking of an article, when no man has been arrested or charged, these requisites must be satisfied:

'*First:* The police officers must have reasonable grounds for believing that a serious offence has been committed — so serious that it is of the first importance that the offenders should be caught and brought to justice.

'*Second:* The police officers must have reasonable grounds for believing that the article in question is either the fruit of the crime (as in the case of stolen goods) or is the instrument by which the crime was committed (as in the case of the axe used by the murderer) or is material evidence to prove the commission of the crime (as in the case of the car used by a bank raider or the saucer used by the criminals in the great train robbery).

'*Third:* The police officers must have reasonable grounds

1. [1970] 1 QB 693 at 705, 708.

to believe that the person in possession of it has himself committed the crime, or is implicated in it, or is accessory to it, or at any rate his refusal must be quite unreasonable.

'*Fourth:* The police must not keep the article, nor prevent its removal, for any longer than is reasonably necessary to complete their investigations or preserve it for evidence. If a copy will suffice, it should be made and the original returned. As soon as the case is over, or it is decided not to go on with it, the article should be returned.

'*Finally:* The lawfulness of the conduct of the police must be judged at the time, and not by what happens afterwards.

'Tested by these criteria, I do not think the police officers are entitled to hold on to these passports or letters. They may have reasonable grounds for believing that the woman has been murdered. But they have not shown reasonable grounds for believing that these passports and letters are material evidence to prove the commission of the murder. All they say is that they are of "evidential value", whatever that may mean. Nor have they shown reasonable grounds for believing that the plaintiffs are in any way implicated in a crime, or accessory to it. In any case, they have held them quite long enough. They have no doubt made photographs of them, and that should suffice.

'It was suggested that a mandatory order should not be made for their return. The case, it was said, should go for trial, and the officers made liable in damages if they are wrong. But I think their affidavits fall so far short of any justification for retention that they should be ordered to return them forthwith. I cannot help feeling that the real reason why the passports have not been returned is because the officers wish to prevent the plaintiffs from leaving this country pending police inquiries. That is not a legitimate ground for holding them. Either they have grounds for arresting them, or they have not. If they have not, the plaintiffs should be allowed to leave — even if it means they are fleeing from the reach of justice. A man's liberty of movement is regarded so highly by the law of England that it is not to be hindered or prevented except on the surest grounds. It must not be taken away on a suspicion which is not grave enough to warrant his arrest'.

2 Search warrants

At common law a search warrant could be issued for stolen goods. But for no other cause.

There are at least a hundred statutes which enable magistrates to issue search warrants for all kinds of offences. Such as for fire-arms, explosives, drugs, counterfeit coins, obscene publications, and so forth. Search warrants are a necessary tool in the war against crime. That is why Parliament has passed those statutes. The Courts have rarely had to consider them. I fancy that that is because the police have only used them when they have reasonable cause to believe that incriminating material is in the house – and they have succeeded in finding it. But there are two leading cases where we had to consider the principles relating to them.

3 The ladies' garments

The first is *Chic Fashions (West Wales) Ltd v Jones*[1]. A factory of Ian Peters Ltd in Leicester was broken into and ladies' garments were stolen. A few weeks later some of those garments were being offered for sale at a shop in Cardiff. The offer was at less than trade prices. The police suspected that the goods stolen from Ian Peters had found their way into the shops of Chic Fashions. So they arranged to search all their shops at one swoop: and also the home of the director. They got search warrants. They did not find any garments of 'Ian Peters' make: but they found garments of other makes which had been stolen previously. They seized them. The director of the shop gave an explanation. It was accepted by the police. They returned the goods to the shop. Thereupon Chic Fashions sued the police for damages. The judge

1. [1968] 2 QB 299.

awarded £500 damages. The police appealed. This is how I dealt with it (at page 309):

'At one time the courts held that the constable could seize only those goods which answered the description given in the warrant. He had to make sure, at his peril, that the goods were the very goods in the warrant. If he seized other goods, not mentioned in the warrant, he was a trespasser in respect of those goods: and not only so, but he was a trespasser on the land itself, a trespasser ab initio, in accordance with the doctrine of the *Six Carpenters' case*[1], which held that, if a man abuse an authority given by the law, he becomes a trespasser ab initio.

'If such had remained the law, no constable would be safe in executing a search warrant. The law as it then stood was a boon to receivers of stolen property and an impediment to the forces of law and order. So much so, that the judges gradually altered it. . . .

. . . .

'Such are the cases. They contain no broad statement of principle: but proceed, in our English fashion, from case to case until the principle emerges. Now the time has come when we must endeavour to state it. We have to consider, on the one hand, the freedom of the individual. The security of his home is not to be broken except for the most compelling reason. On the other hand, we have to consider the interest of society at large in finding out wrongdoers and repressing crime. In these present times, with the ever-increasing wickedness there is about, honest citizens must help the police and not hinder them in their efforts to track down criminals. I look at it in this way: So far as a man's individual liberty is concerned, the law is settled concerning powers of arrest. A constable may arrest him and deprive him of his liberty, if he has reasonable grounds for believing that a felony (now an "arrestable offence") has been committed and that he is the man. I see no reason why goods should be more sacred than persons. In my opinion, when a constable enters a house by virtue of a search warrant

1. (1610) 8 Co Rep 146a.

for stolen goods, he may seize not only the goods which he reasonably believes to be covered by the warrant, but also any other goods which he believes on reasonable grounds to have been stolen and to be material evidence on a charge of stealing or receiving against the person in possession of them or anyone associated with him. Test it this way: Suppose the constable does not find the goods mentioned in the warrant but finds other goods which he reasonably believes to be stolen. Is he to quit the premises and go back to the magistrate and ask for another search warrant to cover these other goods? If he went away, I should imagine that in nine cases out of ten, by the time he came back with a warrant, these other goods would have disappeared. The true owner would not recover them. The evidence of the crime would have been lost. That would be to favour thieves and to discourage honest men. Even if it should turn out that the constable was mistaken and that the other goods were not stolen goods at all, nevertheless so long as he acted reasonably and did not retain them longer than necessary, he is protected. The lawfulness of his conduct must be judged at the time and not by what happens afterwards. I know that at one time a man could be made a trespasser ab initio by the doctrine of relation back. But that is no longer true. The *Six Carpenters' case*[1] was a by-product of the old forms of action. Now that they are buried, it can be interred with their bones.

'In this case, on the agreed facts, the police had reasonable ground for believing the 65 items of clothing to have been stolen and to be material evidence on a criminal charge against the plaintiff company or its officers. So they seized them. On investigation they found out that they were not stolen and they returned them. On the principles I have stated they are not liable'.

4 The military style operation

The second leading case concerns a power of search which Parliament conferred on the officers of the Inland Revenue.

1. (1610) 8 Co Rep 146a.

It was enacted in 1976 in the Finance Act of that year. The
reason was, no doubt, the vast extent of frauds upon the
Revenue. It is said that hundreds of millions of pounds are
lost to the Revenue by reason of these frauds. In order to
try and discover the miscreants — and prosecute them —
Parliament gave a power of search in very wide terms. It was
operated successfully in a dozen or more cases without
challenge. Then action was taken against a group of companies called the Rossminster group and persons closely
connected with them. The Group had been very active in
devising schemes to avoid tax — which they claimed were
lawful. But the Revenue authorities seem to have thought
that the Group did not stop there. They suspected that the
Group and those connected with them had been perpetrating
frauds on a large scale. So they arranged to get search
warrants to search the offices of the Group and the private
houses of individuals connected with the Group. Acting, as
they believed, under the authority of the Statute, they
organised and launched the searches. It was on Friday, 13
July 1979. On the very day the validity of it was challenged
in the Courts. It came quickly before the Divisional Court.
They heard it promptly. On 1 August 1979 they held that
the search was lawful. The Rossminster group immediately
appealed. It was in the vacation. We arranged for it to be
heard at the earliest possible moment. The argument took
three days on 13, 14 and 15 August 1979 and we gave judgment on Thursday 16 August 1979. We held that the Revenue
authorities had acted unlawfully. We quashed the search
warrants. But immediately the Revenue authorities sought
leave to appeal. We gave it at once because of the importance
of this case. So it may be that our decision will be set aside
by the House of Lords. But meanwhile, as it is such a dramatic story, I would set it out as I did in my judgment (the
Rossminster case[1]):

'It was a military style operation. It was carried out by
officers of the Inland Revenue in their war against tax
frauds. Zero hour was fixed for 7.00 a.m. on Friday, 13 July

1. [1979] 3 All ER 385, CA.

116

1979. Everything was highly secret. The other side must not be forewarned. There was a briefing session beforehand. Some 70 officers or more of the Inland Revenue attended. They were given detailed instructions. They were divided into teams each with a leader. Each team had an objective allotted to it. It was to search a particular house or office, marked, I expect, on a map: and to seize any incriminating documents found therein. Each team leader was on the day to be handed a search warrant authorising him and his team to enter the house or office. It would be empowered to use force if need be. Each team was to be accompanied by a police officer. Sometimes more than one. The role of the police was presumably to be silent witnesses: or maybe to let it be known that this was all done with the authority of the law: and that the householder had better not resist — or else!

'Everything went according to plan. On Thursday, 12 July, Mr. Quinlan, the Senior Inspector of the Inland Revenue, went to the Central Criminal Court: and put before a circuit judge — the Common Sergeant — the suspicions which the Revenue held. The circuit judge signed the warrants. The officers made photographs of the warrants, and distributed them to the team leaders. Then in the early morning of Friday, 13 July — the next day — each team started off at first light. Each reached its objective. Some in London. Others in the Home Counties. At 7.00 a.m. there was a knock on each door. One was the home in Kensington of Mr. Ronald Anthony Plummer, a chartered accountant. It was opened by his daughter aged 11. He came downstairs in his dressing-gown. The officers of the Inland Revenue were at the door accompanied by a detective inspector. The householder Mr. Plummer put up no resistance. He let them in. They went to his filing cabinet and removed a large number of files. They went to the safe and took building society passbooks, his children's cheque books and passports. They took his daughter's school report. They went to his bedroom, opened a suitcase, and removed a bundle of papers belonging to his mother. They searched the house. They took personal papers of his wife.

'Another house was the home near Maidstone of Mr. Roy Clifford Tucker, a fellow of the Institute of Chartered Accountants. He was away on business in Guernsey. So his wife opened the door. The officers of the Inland Revenue produced the search warrant. She let them in. She did not know what to do. She telephoned her husband in Guernsey. She told him that they were going through the house taking all the documents they could find. They took envelopes addressed to students who were tenants. They went up to the attic and took papers stored there belonging to Mr. Tucker's brother. They took Mr. Tucker's passport.

'The main attack was reserved for the offices at No. 1 Hanover Square of the Rossminster group of companies of which Mr. Plummer and Mr. Tucker were directors. They were let in by one of the employees. Many officers of the Inland Revenue went in accompanied by police officers. It was a big set of offices with many rooms full of files, papers and documents of all kinds. They took large quantities of them, pushed them into plastic bags, carried them down in the lift, and loaded them into a van. They carried them off to the offices of the Inland Revenue at Melbourne House in the Aldwych. Twelve van loads. They cleared out Mr. Tucker's office completely: and other rooms too. They spent the whole day on it from 7.00 a.m. until 6.30 at night. They did examine some of the documents carefully, but there were so many documents and so many files that they could not examine them all. They simply put a number on each file, included it in a list, and put it into the plastic bag. Against each file they noted the time they did it. It looks as if they averaged one file a minute. They did not stop at files. They took the shorthand notebooks of the typists — I do not suppose they could read them. They took some of the financial newspapers in a bundle. In one case the "top half" of a drawer was taken in the first instalment and the balance of the drawer was taken in the second.

'Another set of offices was next door in St. George Street — I think along the same corridor. It was the office of A.J.R. Financial Services Limited. The director Mr. Hallas was not there, of course, at seven o'clock. He arrived at 9.10 a.m. He found the officers of the Inland Revenue packing the company's files into bags for removal. He said that it amounted to several hundreds of documents. Police officers were in attendance there too.

'At no point did any of the householders make any resistance. They did the only thing open to them. They went off to their solicitors. They saw counsel. They acted very quickly. By the evening they had gone to a judge of the Chancery Division, Mr. Justice Walton, and asked for and obtained an injunction to stop any trespassing on the premises. They telephoned the injunction through to Hanover Square at about a quarter to six at night. The officers thereupon brought the search and seizure to an end. They had, however, by this time practically completed it. So the injunction made very little difference. . . .

'So end the facts. As far as my knowledge of history goes, there has been no search like it — and no seizure like it — in England since that Saturday, 30 April 1763 when the Secretary of State issued a general warrant by which he authorised the King's messengers to arrest John Wilkes and seize all his books and papers. They took everything — all his manuscripts and all papers whatsoever. His pocket-book filled up the mouth of the sack. He applied to the courts. Chief Justice Pratt struck down the general warrant. You will find it all set out in *R v John Wilkes*[1], *Huckle v Money*[2] and *Entick v Carrington*[3]. Chief Justice Pratt said: "To enter a man's house by virtue of a nameless warrant, in order to procure evidence, is worse than the Spanish inquisition; a law under which no Englishman would wish to live an hour: it was a most daring public attack made upon the liberty of the subject".

'Now we have to see in this case whether this warrant was valid or not. It all depends of course upon the statute. . . .
. . . .

1. (1763) 2 Wils 151.
2. (1763) 2 Wils 205.
3. (1765) 2 Wils 275.

'Many will ask: Why has Parliament done this? Why have they allowed this search and seizure by the Revenue officers? It did it here because the Board of Inland Revenue were very worried by the devices used by some wicked people, such as those — and we often see such cases in our courts — who keep two sets of books: one for themselves to use; the other to be shown to the Revenue. Those who make out two invoices. One for the customer. The other to be shown to the taxman. Those who enter into fictitious transactions and write them into their books as genuine. Those who show losses when they have in fact made gains. In the tax evasion pool, there are some big fish who do not stop at tax avoidance. They resort to frauds on a large scale. I can well see that if the legislation were confined — or could be confined — to people of that sort, it would be supported by all honest citizens. Those who defraud the Revenue in this way are parasites who suck out the life-blood of our society. The trouble is that the legislation is drawn so widely that in some hands it might be an instrument of oppression. It may be said that "honest people need not fear: that it will never be used against them: that tax inspectors can be trusted, only to use it in the case of the big, bad frauds". That is an attractive argument, but I would reject it. Once great power is granted, there is a danger of it being abused. Rather than risk such abuse, it is, as I see it, the duty of the courts so to construe the statute as to see that it encroaches as little as possible upon the liberties of the people of England.

. . . .

'I come back to the challenge of the warrant. The challenge which is made here is that it does not specify any particular offence involving fraud. There may be twenty different kinds of fraud, as someone suggested, and this warrant does not specify which one of them is suspected. Each of the deponents, in complaining to the court, complain of this. There is a paragraph which each of them makes in his affidavit:

"Despite requests by my Solicitor so to do, the Inland Revenue have refused to disclose the nature of the offence or offences they have in mind and neither I, nor I verily believe my fellow directors, have the slightest idea what offence or offences they do have in mind, or even who is supposed to have committed it or them".

. . . .

'. . . . When the officers of the Inland Revenue come armed with a warrant to search a man's home or his office, it seems to me that he is entitled to say, "Of what offence do you suspect me? You are claiming to enter my house and to seize my papers". And when they look at the papers and seize them, he should be able to say, "Why are you seizing these papers? Of what offence do you suspect me? What have these to do with your case?" Unless he knows the particular offence charged, he cannot take steps to secure himself or his property. So it seems to me, as a matter of construction of the statute and therefore of the warrant — in pursuance of our traditional role to protect the liberty of the individual — it is our duty to say that the warrant must particularise the specific offence which is charged as being fraud on the tax.

'If this be right, it follows necessarily that this warrant is bad. It should have specified the particular offence of which the man is suspected. On this ground I would hold that certiorari should go to quash the warrant.

. . . .

'So it cannot be that these officers are the people conclusively to decide "whether there is reasonable cause to believe". The courts must be able to exercise some supervision over them. If the courts cannot do so, no one else can. Just see what these officers did here. Mr. Bateson went through the evidence of what they did. Minute by minute. File after file. From their own lists. They could not possibly have had time to examine all these documents or to come to a proper decision as to whether they were reasonably required as evidence. Instead of examining them on the premises, they bundled them into plastic bags and took them off to Melbourne House. . . .

'. . . . I would ask, on what grounds did these officers

121

decide whether or not there was reasonable cause for believing that they would be required in evidence? What about the shorthand notebooks, the diaries, and all that kind of thing — would they be reasonably required? Mr. Davenport said that at this stage the Revenue would not wish to go further than they had. They would not tell us on what grounds they required these documents. At this stage, he said, it is not desirable. He emphasised "at this stage", meaning, I suppose, not until after the criminal proceedings.

'To my mind that is not a sufficient answer. It means that these officers would be exempt from any control by the courts or anyone else until after the criminal proceedings — if there are criminal proceedings — take place. It would mean that for all this time no one would have any control over the operations of the officers of the Inland Revenue who are making this search and seizure. Nothing can be done even by the courts in case they have exceeded their powers. No one can control them.

. . . .

'This brings me to the end. This case has given us much concern. No one would wish that any of those who defraud the Revenue should go free. They should be found out and brought to justice. But it is fundamental in our law that the means which are adopted to this end should be lawful means. A good end does not justify a bad means. The means must not be such as to offend against the personal freedom and the privacy of individuals, and the elemental rights of property. Every man is presumed to be innocent until he is found guilty. If his house is to be searched and his property seized on suspicion of an offence, it must be done by due process of law. And due process involves that there must be a valid warrant specifying the offence of which he is suspected: and the seizure is limited to those things authorised by the warrant. In this case, as I see it, the warrant was invalid for want of particularity: and the search and seizure were not in accordance with anything which was authorised by the warrant. It was an illegal and excessive use of power'.

3 New procedures

Introduction

Apart from Statutes, there have been interesting developments of law. New procedures have been invented which have an analogy with search warrants. Many frauds or other wrongs are committed in secret. The offenders have the papers or the things in their possession. If forewarned they will dispose of them. To prevent this, the courts have had recourse to the flexible remedy of injunction. To show how it works, I must give some examples.

1 The pirates—the *Anton Piller* order

This new procedure was invented by an ingenious member of the Chancery Bar, Mr. Hugh Laddie. He was consulted by the makers of gramophone records. They have the copyright in all kinds of music and earn their living from royalties on records. Yet these recordings can be easily copied: and there is a vast market for the 'pirates' of them. These 'pirates' reproduce the music illicitly on tapes and records. They have a cheap apparatus. The infringing copies are sold by small shopkeepers in poor surroundings. In the first case in 1974 the owners had a copyright in sound recordings of Indian music. They found out that a Mr. Pandit in a small shop in Leicester was selling infringing copies at a very low price. They issued a writ against him. He swore an affidavit in those proceedings. He said that he had only a very few of these records: that he bought them from a Mr. Hajisayed of Dubai in the Persian Gulf with no proper address. Only a convenient

123

Post Office Box Number. He swore to his own innocence and produced a letter to prove it.

The owners of the copyright discovered that that affidavit was a pack of lies: and that Mr. Pandit had forged the letter. They were sure that Mr. Pandit had large quantities of infringing materials on his premises: but, if they went through all the usual legal procedures — and served him with process — those infringing copies could disappear. In Mr. Justice Templeman's phrase, 'the horse will rapidly leave the stable'. So the owners of the copyright made an application — *ex parte* — for an order enabling them to enter on the premises and look for the infringing copies. The judge realised that it appeared 'at first blush, to be a trespass of property and invasion of privacy'. But he made the order, see *EMI v Pandit*[1]. Similarly, orders were made in like cases by other Chancery Judges: until one judge doubted the validity of them. Mr. Laddie then brought a case before us to test the point. It was again *ex parte* — so that the other side knew nothing of it. We looked into it all carefully and upheld the new procedure. It is *Anton Piller KG v Manufacturing Processes Ltd*[2]. That case was not about records, but about drawings and confidential information. I need not go into the details but would turn to my judgment. It will tell you all about the new procedure and its justification (page 59):

'Brightman J . . . refused to order inspection or removal of the documents. He said:

"There is strong prima facie evidence that the defendant company is now engaged in seeking to copy the plaintiffs' components for its own financial profit to the great detriment of the plaintiffs and in breach of the plaintiffs' rights".

'He realised that the defendants might suppress evidence or misuse documentary material, but he thought that that was a risk which must be accepted in civil matters save in extreme cases.

"Otherwise", he said, "it seems to me that an order on the lines sought might become an instrument of oppression,

1. [1975] 1 WLR 302.
2. [1976] Ch 55.

particularly in a case where a plaintiff of big standing and deep pocket is ranged against a small man who is alleged on the evidence of one side only to have infringed the plaintiffs' rights".

'Let me say at once that no court in this land has any power to issue a search warrant to enter a man's house so as to see if there are papers or documents there which are of an incriminating nature, whether libels or infringements of copyright or anything else of the kind. No constable or bailiff can knock at the door and demand entry so as to inspect papers or documents. The householder can shut the door in his face and say "Get out". That was established in the leading case of *Entick v Carrington*[1]. None of us would wish to whittle down that principle in the slightest. But the order sought in this case is not a search warrant. It does not authorise the plaintiffs' solicitors or anyone else to enter the defendants' premises against their will. It does not authorise the breaking down of any doors, nor the slipping in by a back door, nor getting in by an open door or window. It only authorises entry and inspection by the permission of the defendants. The plaintiffs must get the defendants' permission. But it does do this: It brings pressure on the defendants to give permission. It does more. It actually orders them to give permission — with, I suppose, the result that if they do not give permission, they are guilty of contempt of court.

'This may seem to be a search warrant in disguise. . . .

'. . . . It falls to us to consider it on principle. It seems to me that such an order can be made by a judge *ex parte*, but it should only be made where it is essential that the plaintiff should have inspection so that justice can be done between the parties: and when, if the defendant were forewarned, there is a grave danger that vital evidence will be destroyed, that papers will be burnt or lost or hidden, or taken beyond the jurisdiction, and so the ends of justice be defeated: and when the inspection would do no real harm to the defendant or his case.

1. (1765) 2 Wils 275.

'Nevertheless, in the enforcement of this order, the plaintiffs must act with due circumspection. On the service of it, the plaintiffs should be attended by their solicitor, who is an officer of the court. They should give the defendants an opportunity of considering it and of consulting their own solicitor. If the defendants wish to apply to discharge the order as having been improperly obtained, they must be allowed to do so. If the defendants refuse permission to enter or to inspect, the plaintiffs must not force their way in. They must accept the refusal, and bring it to the notice of the court afterwards, if need be on an application to commit.

'You might think that with all these safeguards against abuse, it would be of little use to make such an order. But it can be effective in this way: It serves to tell the defendants that, on the evidence put before it, the court is of opinion that they ought to permit inspection — nay, it orders them to permit — and that they refuse at their peril. It puts them in peril not only of proceedings for contempt, but also of adverse inferences being drawn against them; so much so that their own solicitor may often advise them to comply. We are told that in two at least of the cases such an order has been effective. We are prepared, therefore, to sanction its continuance, but only in an extreme case where there is grave danger of property being smuggled away or of vital evidence being destroyed'.

That case has revolutionised the practice. In a case two years later (*Ex parte Island Records Ltd*[1]) I explained how it worked:

'These "pirates" used to do an enormous trade in infringing copies of recorded music. It was very difficult to catch them. As soon as one small shopkeeper was sued, he got rid of all infringing material. He passed his stock to a fellow pirate: and then declared that he never had any records except the one which the plaintiffs had discovered. This stratagem was, however, defeated by the enterprise of Mr. Laddie. He persuaded the judges of the Chancery Division to make an order — *ex parte* — on the shopkeeper before the

1. [1978] Ch 122 at 133.

writ is served. This order is served on him, with the writ, in the presence of a solicitor. It catches the pirate unawares — before he has had time to destroy or dispose of his infringing stock or his incriminating papers. It requires him to disclose all relevant material that he has. The order "freezes" the stock which he has and enables the plaintiff to inspect it. The order contained safeguards to see that no injustice was done. The first reported case was the order made by Templeman J in *EMI Ltd v Pandit*[1]. The practice was confirmed and consolidated by the decision of this court in *Anton Piller KG v Manufacturing Processes Ltd*[2]. The effect of these *ex parte* orders has been dramatic. When served with them, the shop-keepers have acknowledged their wrongdoing and thrown their hand in. So useful are these orders that they are in daily use — not only in cases of infringement of copyright, but also in passing-off cases, and other cases. They are called *"Anton Piller"* orders'.

2 The bootleggers

The essence of the *Anton Piller* case was that the owners of the copyright sued for infringement of copyright. That case did not apply in favour of people who did not own the copyright. Such as 'pop artistes' who perform a piece of music but do not own the copyright in it. They were in difficulty because it was said that they had no property right on which to rest their claim. The difficulty was so serious that it was only by 2 to 1 that we decided in their favour. Lord Justice Shaw dissented. He is so full of good sense that it makes me doubt my own judgment. But this is what I said in *Ex parte Island Records Ltd*[3]:

'If you would like a caption for this case, I can suggest it. It is "Pop Artistes want to stop Bootleggers". It needs explanation for the innocents. Take a popular group who play and sing live in a theatre or in a broadcasting studio. They give

1. [1975] 1 WLR 302.
2. [1976] Ch 55.
3. [1978] Ch 122 at 132.

an exciting performance. This performance is transmitted on to a tape by a recording company. The company afterwards make records of it and sell them to the public. But there is a person in the audience or beside the wireless set who is listening to the performance. He has in his hand or his pocket one of the latest scientific devices. It is a tiny machine by which he records on tape this exciting performance. It is called a condenser microphone. Having recorded it on the one tape, he then uses the tape to make hundreds of copies and sell them in the form of cassettes and cartridges or gramophone records. Sometimes these are poor in quality. Sometimes they are as good as the records made by the recording companies themselves. They are sold to the public by small shopkeepers at cut prices and eat into the sales of the recording companies. The performers suffer also: because they receive royalties from the recording companies according to the number sold.

'The performers, however, have no copyright in their performance: nor have the recording companies. No matter how brilliant the performance – which no one else could rival – nevertheless it is so intangible, so fleeting, so ethereal, that it is not protected by the law of copyright. The actual musical work which they play or sing may itself be the subject of copyright, but the performers have no right in that musical work itself. It may be out of copyright. It may be the work of an old composer who died long ago. Or it may be the copyright of a modern composer or owner, who has already been paid his due. The important thing to notice is that the performers themselves have no copyright.

'No matter that the performers have no copyright, nevertheless the making of these secret tapes and records – and the selling of them – is quite illegal if it is done without the written consent of the performers. It is a criminal offence, punishable by fine or imprisonment. Those who engage in this trade are called "bootleggers". That is a term which was coined in the United States 100 years ago. Those engaged in illicit trading in liquor used to hide it in the upper part of their tall boots – the leg of the boot.

128

. . . .

'Now we have the question whether *Anton Piller* orders can be made against bootleggers. To a layman there would seem no difference between pirates and bootleggers. If an *Anton Piller* order can be made against a pirate, it should be possible, too, against a bootlegger. . . .

. . . .

'In the present case both the performers and the recording companies have, to my mind, private rights and interests which they are entitled to have protected from unlawful interference. The recording companies have the right to exploit the records made by them of the performance. The performers have the right to the royalty payable to them out of those records. Those rights are buttressed by the contracts between the recording companies and the performers. They are rights in the nature of rights of property. Both the recording companies and the performers suffer severe damage if those rights are unlawfully interfered with. Suppose that the bootlegger in the audience had in his hand or his pocket – instead of a recording device – a distorting device: and by it he could introduce a squeak or a screech into the musical performance: and thus ruin its commercial value. No one could doubt that the recording company and the performers could bring an action to stop him and claim damages. That illustration shows that they have a private right which they are entitled to have protected: and this is so, no matter whether the interference be by means of a tortious act or a criminal act. The wrongdoer cannot take advantage of his own crime so as to damage a private individual with impunity.

. . . .

'So my conclusion is that the courts have jurisdiction to grant an *Anton Piller* order in regard to bootleggers, just as they have in regard to pirates. I am confirmed in this view by the fact that it carries out to the full the recommendations of the Committee presided over by Whitford J[1]. The granting of the *"Anton Piller"* order is subject to the safeguards mentioned in the report of that case. I would, therefore,

1. Cmnd. 6732 (1977), paras. 412 (iii), 414 (iv), 419 (iv).

allow this appeal and remit the case to the judge for him to deal with bootleggers just as is done in the case of pirates'.

Part four
The *Mareva* injunction

Introduction

In most countries of the world a creditor can impound the property of his debtor – at the outset – long before he has got judgment against the debtor: and then have the property – or its equivalent – retained as security for payment of the debt in case he afterwards gets judgment. This process is called in the French language *saisie conservatoire*. I suppose it means literally a 'conservative seizure' or 'a seizure of assets so as to conserve them for the creditor in case he should afterwards get judgment'. But whatever it means, there is no doubt that for the last 150 years English law has known no such thing. Scottish law had something of the kind. But English law had nothing. In England a creditor could seize nothing until he got judgment against the debtor. This was very serious for the creditor. Some time always elapses between the issue of a writ and the obtaining of a judgment. All sorts of delaying tactics can be put up by a debtor. Meanwhile he can get rid of his assets in all kinds of ways. A familiar device is to put them into the name of his wife: and say that they always belonged to her. To overcome such devices, there is machinery – after judgment – to make him bankrupt and to set aside the device as being a fraud on the creditor. Such machinery is not very effective – even against an English debtor. But it is quite useless if the debtor absconds and goes off to a foreign country taking his assets with him: or if he lives in a foreign country and removes his assets outside England.

1 We introduce the process

1 The start off

On 22 May 1975 a case came before us which started off the greatest piece of judicial law reform in my time.

The facts were simple. Japanese shipowners entered into charterparties with two Greek gentlemen. The slump in shipping overtook them. They did not pay the hire. They disappeared. Their office in the Piraeus was closed. But they had funds with a bank in London. The Japanese owners feared that the two Greek gentlemen would transfer those funds to Switzerland or some other country. It could be done in a moment by a telegraphic transfer. So their solicitors issued a writ for service out of the jurisdiction — and immediately — before service — applied to the Court here for an injunction to stop the funds being removed outside the jurisdiction. The judge refused it on the simple ground that nothing of that kind could be done in England. The Japanese shipowners immediately came to our Court and we immediately granted the injunction. I put it in these words in *Nippon Yusen Kaisha v Karageorgis*[1]:

'We are told that an injunction of this kind has never been granted before. It has never been the practice of the English courts to seize assets of a defendant in advance of judgment or to restrain the disposal of them. We were told that Chapman J in chambers recently refused such an application. In this case also Donaldson J refused it. We know, of course, that the practice on the continent of Europe is different.

1. [1975] 1 WLR 1093 at 1094.

134

'It seems to me that the time has come when we should revise our practice. There is no reason why the High Court or this court should not make an order such as is asked for here. It is warranted by section 45 of the Supreme Court of Judicature (Consolidation) Act 1925 which says that the High Court may grant a mandamus or injunction or appoint a receiver by an interlocutory order in all cases in which it appears to the court to be just or convenient so to do. It seems to me that this is just such a case. There is a strong prima facie case that the hire is owing and unpaid. If an injunction is not granted, these moneys may be removed out of the jurisdiction and the shipowners will have the greatest difficulty in recovering anything. Two days ago we granted an injunction *ex parte* and we should continue it'.

2 The *Mareva* itself

That was on 22 May 1975. The news of it soon got round. The practitioners in the Commercial Court are an expert body. The solicitors are very efficient. The Bar is first-class. But they are a small body. There was no need to wait for the case to be reported. I am quite sure that by that afternoon every commercial set of chambers in The Temple buzzed with it.

Four weeks later, on 23 June 1975, came the case which gave its name to this new procedure – *Mareva v International Bulkcarriers*[1]. Shipowners let their vessel, the *Mareva*, to time-charterers on terms which required hire to be paid half-monthly in advance. The charterers defaulted on the third instalment. But there was money in a London bank in their name. It had been paid to them by the Government of India as freight for the voyage: and was money which the time-charterers should use to pay the hire. They had not paid it. On this occasion Mr. Rix drew our attention to some cases in the last century – in the Court of Appeal – which showed the then view that no injunction could be granted before judgment. But we put them on one side. I said (at page 510):

1. [1975] 2 Lloyd's Rep 509.

'If it appears that the debt is due and owing — and there is a danger that the debtor may dispose of his assets so as to defeat it before judgment — the court has jurisdiction in a proper case to grant an interlocutory injunction so as to prevent him disposing of those assets. It seems to me that this is a proper case for the exercise of this jurisdiction'.

Those two cases ended there. The defendants never applied to discharge the injunctions. The reason was because the money was undoubtedly due: they submitted to judgment: and the funds in the Bank were used to pay it. So the procedure had proved its usefulness.

3 Both sides are heard

But the two cases could not be considered to be authority at this stage. The applications had been made *ex parte*. Only the creditor had been heard. No argument had been made on the other side. So we had to wait for a case where both sides could be heard. It took nearly two years. Then in March 1977 came *Rasu v Perusahaan ('Pertamina')*[1]. It arose out of events in the Far East. Rasu, a Liberian company, issued a writ against Pertamina, an Indonesian state-owned company. Rasu claimed damages of nearly £2 million sterling for breach of a charterparty. Rasu sought to attach the assets of Pertamina in many countries: but Pertamina had been busy getting rid of its assets or putting them out of the reach of its creditors. At length Rasu found there were assets of Pertamina in England. These assets were in Liverpool. They were lying at the West Gladstone Dock awaiting shipment. They were parts of equipment for making a floating fertiliser plant. Rasu applied for a *Mareva* injunction to stop this equipment being taken out of the jurisdiction of the Court. On the *ex parte* application Kerr J granted the injunction. Pertamina applied to discharge it. It was a time when we were so busy in the Court of Appeal that we could only spare two Lords Justices

1. [1978] QB 644.

136

for interlocutory applications. By 'interlocutory applications' we mean applications of a minor or interim nature – as distinct from 'final appeals' which decide the rights of the parties finally. So there were only two of us – Lord Justice Orr and me – to decide this important case. The case was argued for the plaintiffs by Mr. Nicholas Phillips, then a junior but since a silk of first quality. For Pertamina there was Michael Mustill, a Queen's Counsel of outstanding merit, now a Judge. He took the line which is often pursued nowadays with success. He submitted that it was wrong for the Judges to make any reform in our law. It should be left to Parliament. This I rejected in these words (page 661):

'Mr. Mustill urged us not to introduce it here by decision of the judges but to wait for legislation by Parliament, so that the implications could be considered on a wider plane. That was the sort of submission which was urged upon the House of Lords in *Miliangos v George Frank (Textiles) Ltd*[1] about judgments in foreign currency. It was accepted by Lord Simon of Glaisdale, but the House rejected it. They upheld the new procedure there which we started. As there, so here. It is a field of law reform in which the judges can proceed step by step. They can try out a new procedure and see how it works. That is better than long-drawn-out discussions elsewhere'.

I made a historical and comparative survey of the seizure of assets before judgment. It is so interesting that I would repeat it here for you (page 657):

'. . . . It is said that this new procedure was never known to the law of England. But that is not correct. In former times it was much used in the City of London by a process called foreign attachment. It was originally used so as to compel the defendant to appear and to give bail to attend: but it was extended to all cases when he was not within the jurisdiction. Under it, if the defendant was not to be found within the jurisdiction of the court, the plaintiff was enabled

1. [1976] AC 443.

instantly, as soon as the plaint was issued, to attach any effects of the defendant, whether money or goods, to be found within the jurisdiction of the court. It was described in detail by Bohun in 1723 in his book on the customs of London, *Privilegia Londini* 3rd ed., pp. 253–289: but brought up to date by Pulling in 1842 in *The Laws, Customs, Usages and Regulations of the City and Port of London* 2nd ed., pp. 187–192. He describes the origin and the reasons for it, and it is well worth noting. He says:

"This mode of proceeding, which seems to have prevailed at a very early period in London, as in other Roman provinces, was always considered extremely important to the citizens as a commercial people, who, having given credit to a trader, might be debarred of their remedy by his going out of the jurisdiction of their courts, though at the same time he might have left ample effects behind him in the hands of third parties. . . . This customary mode of proceeding still exists in other ancient cities and towns in England, as Bristol, Exeter, Lancaster, as well as in Scotland, and Jersey, and in most maritime towns on the continent of Europe. In France it is called *saisie arret*, and in Scotland it is termed arrestment . . .".

'. . . . When our citizens of London and Bristol went out to the United States of America and settled there they took with them this process of foreign attachment. This was stated by the Supreme Court of the United States in *Ownbey v Morgan*[1] approving a leading authority, *Drake on Attachment*, which says:

"This custom . . . was doubtless known to our ancestors, when they sought a new home on the Western continent; and its essential principle, brought hither by them, has, in varied forms, become incorporated into the legal systems of all our states".

'This incorporation was first done by the judges but afterwards incorporated into the laws of the various states by legislative enactments, as in the case of the State of Delaware there considered. It was adopted throughout as a remedy for

1. (1921) 256 US 94.

collecting debts due from non-resident or absconding debtors
. . . .

'In the extract which I have read from Pulling he says that the same process was available in most maritime towns on the continent of Europe. There it has survived most vigorously and is in force everywhere today. It is called in France *saisie conservatoire*. It is applied universally on the continent. It enables the seizure of assets so as to preserve them for the benefit of the creditor. Very often the debtor lodges security and gets the assets released.

'Now that we have joined the Common Market, it would be appropriate that we should follow suit, at any rate in regard to defendants not within the jurisdiction. By so doing we should be fulfilling one of the requirements of the Treaty of Rome. That is the harmonisation of the laws of the member countries'.

Then I turned to the two earlier cases and said of them (page 660):

'The two cases of *Nippon Yusen Kaisha v Karageorgis*[1] and *Mareva v International Bulkcarriers*[2] are part of the evolutionary process. This court was there presented with sets of facts which called aloud for the intervention of the court by injunction. Study those facts and you will see that it was both just and convenient that the courts should restrain the debtor from removing his funds from London. Unless an interlocutory injunction were granted, *ex parte*, the debtor could, and probably would, by a single telex or telegraphic message, deprive the shipowner of the money to which he was plainly entitled. So just and so convenient, indeed, is the procedure that it has been constantly invoked since in the commercial court with the approval of all the judges and users of that court. Now, after full argument, I hold that those cases were rightly decided. . .'.

But in the case of *Rasu v Pertamina* both sides were accusing one another so much that I said (page 662):

1. [1975] 1 WLR 1093.
2. [1975] 2 Lloyd's Rep 509.

'. . . the situation is such that I do not think it would be proper in this case for equity to intervene to assist one side or the other. I am tempted to say, "A plague on both your houses".

. . . .

'. . . this is not a case in which an injunction should be granted to restrain the defendants in the use or disposal of the goods at Liverpool. I agree with the judge in the result . . . . I think the courts have a discretion, in advance of judgment, to issue an injunction to restrain the removal of assets — whether the defendant is within the jurisdiction or outside it. This discretion should not be fettered by rigid rules. It should be exercised when it appears to the court to be just and convenient. . .'.

Although I say it, that decision was a good way of getting things done. By our words we did much to establish the *Mareva* injunction as a new principle — but by our decision we avoided any appeal to the House of Lords. We decided on the merits in favour of the defendants — thus precluding any appeal by them: but we made it clear that that new principle was to be available in future in English law.

2 We are reversed

1 The *Siskina* sinks without trace

Our self-satisfaction was short-lived. Two months later, in May 1977, there came a case, *The Siskina*[1], where we applied the *Mareva* principle only to find our decision reversed by the House of Lords. I have suffered many reversals but never so disappointing as this one. Particularly because I felt that their decision was unjust. It was unjust to buyers of cargo in the Middle East. The story is so dramatic that I will take it from my judgment in the Court of Appeal (page 231):

'The *Siskina* is now sunk to the bottom of the Mediterranean Sea. In her lifetime she was a motor-vessel owned by a one-ship Panamanian company: but she was managed by Greeks in Piraeus. Early last year (i.e. 1976) she was chartered by an Italian firm for a voyage from North Italy to the Red Sea. She arrived at the port of Carrara on the Gulf of Genoa and took on a cargo of general merchandise. Six thousand tons of it. We are much concerned with this cargo. It came from the industrial north of Italy and was destined for the rich land of Saudi Arabia. There were marble slabs and tiles for the wealthy homes. Refrigerators and gas cookers for the kitchens. And blankets in thousands for the cold nights. All to be carried to the port of Jeddah on the Red Sea. So the cargo was a very mixed bag. Many different parcels from many different sellers for many different consignees.

'The buyers in Saudi Arabia had paid for all this cargo in advance. They had bought it from the sellers in North Italy

1. [1977] 2 Lloyd's Rep 230.

on c.i.f. terms by means of irrevocable letters of credit. So they had not only paid the price of the goods themselves. They had in addition paid the freight for the voyage and also the insurance to cover it. All the documents were in order. . . . .

'The vessel, however, never got to Jeddah or anywhere near it. She went through the Mediterranean till she was near the entrance to the Suez Canal. There she stopped. . . . So the *Siskina* waited outside the entrance to the Canal. She waited there for over four weeks — from 6 March 1976 to 6 April 1976.

'. . . . The ship-owning company ordered the master to turn back and go to Cyprus and unload the cargo there. This was not the first occasion of the kind. We are told that during the last year there have been about 20 cases in which vessels, due for discharge in the Middle East, have been diverted to Cyprus. They have there discharged their cargoes rather than carry them to their proper destinations. They pay scant regard to their obligations to the cargo-owners.

'See what happened in this very case. The vessel went back to the port of Limassol in Cyprus. . . .

'. . . . Soon afterwards the cargo was unloaded. The marble tiles and slabs were left in the open and suffered a lot of breakage and chipping. Machinery was left out and was damaged by rain. Other goods were taken to warehouses. The value of the cargo was, we are told, some $5,000,000.

'Soon after the discharge, the vessel about 20 April 1976, left Limassol in ballast with no cargo. She has never been heard of since. All we are told is that six weeks later, on 2 June 1976, she sank near Astipalaia Island and became a total loss. That island is one of the Dodecanese on the way from Cyprus to Greece. We know of no reason why she sank. All we know is that the ship-owning company have made a claim on the London underwriters: and that the sum payable for the loss of the vessel will be more than $750,000.

'The cargo-owners knew nothing of all this. They were merchants in Saudi Arabia, not well-versed in the intricacies of transport by sea. They made inquiries of the shippers, who inquired of the charterers. It was only on 31 May 1976 that their lawyers in Genoa first heard that the goods had been taken to Cyprus, unloaded there and arrested by the ship-owning company alleging a lien for freight. They immediately instructed lawyers in Cyprus: but by that time the vessel had disappeared without trace. They also instructed lawyers in London.

. . . .

'In England the cargo-owners were anxious about the insurance moneys which were payable in London to the ship-owners for the loss of the *Siskina*. The ship-owning company had no assets except these insurance moneys: and the cargo-owners (or their insurers) did not want these moneys paid over to the shipowners, because they would then be beyond reach. So the cargo-owners on 2 July 1976 drafted a writ in the Commercial Court against the shipowners. . . .

'On that self-same day, 2 July 1976, the cargo-owners went before Mr. Justice Mocatta. He gave the leave asked and granted an injunction in those very terms to restrain the ship-owners from disposing of the insurance moneys. . . .

. . . .

'So the position today is that goods of much value are still languishing on shore in Cyprus. I suppose about $3,000,000 worth. Some in the open exposed to the weather. Others in warehouses in unknown conditions. Storage charges are running up day by day. These will have to be paid before the goods are released: and the cargo-owners will have to pay the cost of carrying them to Jeddah: although they have paid it once already. . . .

'The shipowners are a "one-ship" company, whose one ship the *Siskina* is sunk beneath the waves. They have no other ship. They have no business and have no intention of carrying on any business. They have no assets except the insurance moneys of $750,000 payable by London under-writers for the loss of the *Siskina*.

'The cargo-owners have a claim against the shipowners for substantial damages for failing to carry the goods to Jeddah

143

as promised by the bills of lading, all marked "Freight Pre-paid": and for damages for wrongfully diverting the vessel to Limassol and wrongfully discharging the cargo there under an unwarranted claim of lien. The damages are put at some $250,000, and are no doubt increasing daily.

'The cargo-owners want the insurance moneys of $750,000 retained in England — or a sufficient part of it — until their claim for damages is settled. Otherwise they are afraid — with good reason — that the $750,000 will be paid out to the ship-owners and deposited in Switzerland, or in some foreign land: and the cargo-owners will have no chance of getting anything for all the damage they have suffered.

. . . .

'. . . . To my mind this case comes . . . within the principle of the *Mareva* case. I would, therefore . . . grant an injunction to restrain the removal of the insurance moneys (or such part of them as would suffice to cover the claim of the cargo-owners) . . . .

'It was suggested that this course is not open to us because it would be legislation: and that we should leave the law to be amended by the Rules Committee. But see what this would mean: The ship-owning company would be able to decamp with the insurance moneys and the cargo-owners would have to whistle for any redress. To wait for the Rules Committee would be to shut the stable door after the steed has been stolen. And who knows that there will ever again be another horse in the stable? Or another ship sunk and insurance moneys here? I ask, Why should the Judges wait for the Rules Committee? The Judges have an inherent jurisdiction to lay down the practice and procedure of the Courts: and we can invoke it now to restrain the removal of these insurance moneys. To the timorous souls I would say in the words of William Cowper:

Ye fearful saints, fresh courage take,
The clouds ye so much dread
are big with mercy, and shall break
In blessings on your head.

'Instead of "saints", read "Judges". Instead of "mercy", read "justice". And you will find a good way to law reform . . .'.

2 We are sunk too like the *Siskina*

Alas, the shipowners appealed to the House of Lords: and we were overruled. I had a fear that the Lords would overrule the *Mareva* principle itself – that they would say that we had been indulging in a piece of law reform which was outside our province. If they had done so, it would have much upset the solicitors of the City of London – who had found it very useful. But the skill of Mr. Anthony Lloyd QC saved us from that disaster. He did not challenge the *Mareva* principle itself. He only submitted that it did not apply to the *Siskina* case on particular grounds: and the House decided it on very narrow grounds. Yet they could not resist the opportunity of rebuking the Court of Appeal. Lord Hailsham of St. Marylebone made observations with which two others expressly agreed[1]:

'. . . . The jurisdiction of the Rules Committee is statutory, and for Judges of first instance or on appeal to pre-empt its functions is, at least in my opinion, for the Courts to usurp the function of the legislature. . . .
'. . . . To follow Lord Denning MR in his invitation to pre-empt its counsels is . . . to usurp the function of a legislative body entrusted by Parliament with a particular task. . . . Even if such a usurpation were legitimate, which in my view it is not, it would in my judgment be highly undesirable'.

3 But not without trace

The decision in the *Siskina* case was on such narrow grounds that it did not shake the solicitors of the City of London at all. They kept on course. *The Siskina* was decided on 26 October 1977. Eighteen months later, in May 1979, Mustill J

1. [1979] AC 210 at 261.

145

(who had much experience of the *Mareva* injunction both at the Bar and on the Bench) said:

'The use of the remedy greatly increased. Far from being exceptional it has now become commonplace. At present, applications are being made at the rate of about 20 per month. Almost all are granted'.

Mustill J made that remark in the course of a case which marked the next step in development. It was *Third Chandris Corporation v Unimarine*[1]. It was decided by us as recently as 24 May 1979. Three owners of three vessels had claims against a big group of charterers. The claims were not met promptly. The shipowners were anxious about the position. They applied for and obtained *Mareva* injunctions. The charterers applied to discharge them. They said they had good defences to the claims: and they were such a substantial group that there was no fear of their not meeting any sums which might be found due. Despite this assertion Mustill J continued the *Mareva* injunctions and we affirmed his decision. We had to consider *The Siskina* and I said that it did not impugn the *Mareva* principle (page 135):

'It is just four years now since we introduced here the procedure known as *Mareva* injunctions. All the other legal systems of the world have a similar procedure. It is called in the civil law *saisie conservatoire*. It has been welcomed in the City of London and has proved extremely beneficial. It enables a creditor in a proper case to stop his debtor from parting with his assets pending trial. Two years ago, the House of Lords had this procedure under their close consideration. It was in *The Siskina*[2]. If the House had any doubts about our jurisdiction in the matter, I should have expected them to give voice to them, rather than let the legal profession continue in error. But none of their Lordships did cast any doubt on it. Impressed with the unanimity of his colleagues, Lord Hailsham of St. Marylebone said, at page 261:

1. [1979] 3 WLR 122.
2. [1979] AC 210.

"Since the House is in no way casting doubt on the validity
of the new practice by its decision in the instant appeal, I do
not wish in any way to do so myself. . .".'

I set out some guidelines on the practice and continued
(page 138):

'In setting out those guidelines, I hope we shall do nothing
to reduce the efficacy of the present practice. In it speed is
of the essence. *Ex parte* is of the essence. If there is delay, or
if advance warning is given, the assets may well be removed
before the injunction can bite. It is rather like the new
injunction in Chancery, the *Anton Piller* injunction (*Anton
Piller KG v Manufacturing Processes Ltd*[1]), which has proved
equally beneficial. That must be done speedily *ex parte*
before the incriminating material is removed. So here in
Mareva injunctions before the assets are removed. The
solicitors of the City of London can, I believe, continue their
present practice so long as they do it with due regard to their
responsibilities: and so long as the judges exercise a wise
discretion so as to see that the procedure is not abused'.

4 An English-based defendant

In the case I also sought to record an extension of the *Mareva*
principle to an English-based defendant[2] :

'The House left open the position of a plaintiff making a
claim against an English-based defendant. Lord Hailsham of
St. Marylebone said significantly, at page 261 (of the *Siskina*
case[3]):
"Either the position of a plaintiff making a claim against
an English-based defendant will have to be altered or the
principle of the *Mareva* cases will have to be modified".
'In the recent case of *Chartered Bank v Daklouche* (unreported) 16 March 1979, CA, we did apply the *Mareva* injunction
to an English-based defendant. A wife came from Abu Dhabi

1. [1976] Ch 55.
2. [1979] 3 WLR 122 at 136.
3. [1979] AC 210.

in the Persian Gulf to England. She bought a large house in Hampshire, and had £70,000 in a bank in England in her own name. Mocatta J granted a *Mareva* injunction, and this court affirmed it. I said:

"The law should be that there is jurisdiction to grant a *Mareva* injunction even though the defendant may be served here. If he makes a fleeting visit, or if there is a danger that he may abscond, or that the assets or moneys may disappear and be taken out of the reach of the creditors, a *Mareva* injunction can be granted. Here is this £70,000 lying in a bank in England, which can be removed at the stroke of a pen from England outside the reach of the creditors" '.

It now appears that meanwhile on 21 December 1978 Lloyd J had held that a *Mareva* injunction could not be granted against an English-based defendant, see *The Agrabele*[1]. But I hope that our later case of 16 March 1979 (mentioned above) has dispelled any suggestion that there is any jurisdictional bar. It should be possible for a *Mareva* injunction to be granted against an English-based defendant if there is any danger that he may abscond or remove his assets.

5 A man is decapitated

The principle is growing apace. Two months later, in July 1979, it was introduced into a very different type of case. Not a ship, nor a charterparty. But an aircraft and a personal injury. It was *Ruth Allen v Jamba (Nigeria) Airways*[2]. A light aeroplane — taking only four people — was on the ground at a small aerodrome near Watford. It was owned by a Nigerian company and was about to leave on its way back to Nigeria. Before the passengers embarked the pilot tested the engine. He started it up. Soon afterwards the passengers came across to get aboard. The first man had his head caught in the revolving propeller. He was decapitated and killed. The

1. [1979] 2 Lloyd's Rep 117.
2. (1979) 20 July (not yet reported).

aircraft did not take off that evening. The pilot waited a week or two for the inquest. After the inquest the pilot said he was going off to Nigeria that evening. The solicitor for the widow feared that, once the aircraft got away, his client would have little chance of getting any damages. So he acted very quickly. He got counsel to telephone a Judge of the High Court at his home. The Judge granted a *Mareva* injunction. The Nigerian company afterwards applied to discharge it. They said that they were a big commercial group in Nigeria, that they were insured with a substantial Nigerian insurance corporation. Despite all these assurances we continued the *Mareva* injunction. It is an important case for two reasons: first, the widow's claim was by no means sure to succeed. Her husband may have been a good deal to blame. Second, it is parallel to the arrest of a ship *in rem*. This is what I said:

'This is the first case we have had of a personal injury – it is a fatal accident case – where a *Mareva* injunction has been sought. The nearest parallel is a ship in an English port where there is an accident causing personal injury or death. It has been settled for centuries that the claimant can bring an action *in rem* and arrest the ship. She is not allowed to leave the port until security is provided so as to ensure that the claim will be duly met.

'The question is whether a similar jurisdiction can be exercised in regard to an aircraft. In principle I see no reason why it should not, except that it is to be done by a *Mareva* injunction instead of an action *in rem*. . . .

'I can see no reason . . . . as is done in shipping cases all over the world – why security should not be given in the way of a bond or an undertaking. . . . If the Nigerian company is of such high standing as we are told it is: if they are ready to accept any liability as we are told they will, it seems to me that a bank or an insurance company of standing in this country would back the Nigerian company. . . . The aircraft must not be removed from the jurisdiction or from the aerodrome until further order'.

6 Recommendations thus far ignored

In all the cases we have heard about the *Mareva* injunction, we have never been referred to an important Report made over ten years ago. It was made by a Committee presided over by Mr. Justice Payne on the *Enforcement of Judgment Debts*[1]. They gave an illustration which I wish we had had before us in the various cases. It makes a convincing case for a *Mareva* injunction against an English-based defendant. It is in paragraph 1252:

'Under modern conditions of travel, particularly as the cost of air travel is now within the means of many a debtor, the risk of goods and chattels, or substantial sums of money being taken out of the country is greatly increased. It is possible to imagine countless circumstances in which a power to restrain a debtor could be justified but one will suffice. A debtor may buy valuable jewellery on credit, ignore demands for payment and ignore a writ or summons. The jeweller may not know where the jewellery is. If he happens to discover that the debtor has booked an air passage and proposes to leave England a few days later and before any progress can be made with the action which has been commenced, is there anyone who would argue in these days that the court should not have power to order that the debtor should not remove the jewellery from the jurisdiction or otherwise dispose of it?'

The Committee followed this by a recommendation in paragraph 1253 that the Court should have power, on the application of a creditor *before* or *after judgment*, to make an order restraining a debtor from removing property out of the jurisdiction or otherwise dealing with it.

Recently another Committee has been sitting under the chairmanship of Mr. Justice Kerr, a most able Judge (now Chairman of the Law Commission) about the enforcement of debts within the European Common Market. That too has, I believe, recommended that a procedure equivalent to *saisie conservatoire* should be available in England just as

1. Cmnd. 3909.

150

it is in the other countries of the Common Market. It should be available so as to prevent the removal of assets, not only by persons outside the jurisdiction of the English Courts, but also by English-based defendants: and it should be available even though there is no cause of action in the English Courts but only in another country of the Common Market. Thus overruling the decision of the House of Lords in *The Siskina.*

I know that these recommendations are now under consideration by those responsible for legislation. I hope that a Bill will soon be introduced to give effect to them. Even if such a Bill is delayed, I hope that the Courts may of themselves develop their own jurisdiction so as to be ahead of the Legislature. But they cannot, of course, overrule the House of Lords in *The Siskina* – without the help of Parliament.

Part five

Entrances and exits

Introduction

In recent times England has been invaded – not by enemies – nor by friends – but by those who seek England as a haven. In their own countries there are poverty, disease and no homes. In England there is social security – a national health service and guaranteed housing – all to be had for the asking without payment and without working for it. Once here, each seeks to bring his relatives to join him. So they multiply exceedingly.

In their own countries, those invaders are low in the social scale. In contrast there are wealthy residents here who leave England – not because they have any complaint against it – but because they seek to avoid the taxes payable by them. They are so numerous that we have a sobriquet for them. They are 'tax-exiles'. These stay away for so long as necessary to be secure for tax relief: and then, when it suits them, return.

Allied to them, there are men of business who form companies in small islands or tiny countries overseas where they will be exempt from the strictness of our company laws and from the heaviness of our taxes. 'Tax-havens' they are called. These companies do not carry on any business in those islands or tiny territories. They have no assets there. But they carry on huge 'offshore operations'. They own ships or charter them. They own businesses and make profits. But by international law (recognised by our municipal law) these companies are separate legal entities. They are not bound to render any accounts to anyone. There is virtually no control over them. The real persons who operate them are not liable for their debts or liabilities. When it comes to the 'crunch' — when they are liable to pay debts or taxes — there is no way of getting at their assets.

Whenever counsel tell us: 'It is a company registered in Liechtenstein or the Cayman Islands', I ask naïvely: 'Why is that?' As if I did not know. Whereas, in 99 cases out of 100, it is to cover up something or other or to avoid some liability or another.

1 The common law about aliens

Introduction

In the last 25 years there has been much concern about the entry of immigrants into England. Previously there was little concern. No restriction was placed on immigrants either by the Common Law or by Statute. So much so that England might well be regarded as the most 'liberal' of all the countries in the world. Much of this law remains so far as aliens are concerned. So I have endeavoured to set out some of the leading cases. They illustrate the importance of our writ of habeas corpus. Case after case was decided on an application for the writ.

1 The 'black' is set free

The most celebrated case in our books on Commonwealth citizens is undoubtedly that of the slave James Somerset. It was decided in 1772. At that time the Crown still had jurisdiction over the colonies of Virginia and Jamaica. Many gentlemen had gone from England to own and run sugar plantations there. (George Washington's grandfather went to Virginia. George himself, who never told a lie, had 49 slaves on his estate at Mount Vernon in 1760. One of my ancestors, Newdigate Poyntz, went to St. Kitts. The surname Poyntz still survives there). Galleys had brought slaves from Africa to those colonies to work in the plantations. By the laws there the planters were authorised to trade in those slaves. They were goods and chattels and, as such, saleable

157

and sold. The current price was £50 a slave. The law of England at one time recognised those laws as valid and applicable even in England. Many planters had acted on that footing. They had brought slaves back with them on their visits to England. In 1749 many planters brought a petition before Lord Hardwicke, the Lord Chancellor, especially to know whether a slave was freed by becoming a Christian. That great Judge held that a slave was not free by coming into England or by being baptised a Christian. The reason given was that the slaves could be trusted whereas the whites could not:

'Tis necessary the master should bring them over: for they cannot trust the whites either with the stores or the navigating of the vessel'.

That opinion was endorsed by another great Judge, Lord Talbot, then Attorney- and Solicitor-General.

But in 1772 that opinion was challenged before Lord Mansfield. James Somerset was a slave who had been purchased from the African coast and taken in a galley to Jamaica where he had been purchased by Mr. Stewart. His master brought him over to England and intended to take him back. James Somerset refused to go. Mr. Stewart took him by force and put him on board a vessel, the 'Ann and Mary', of which Captain Knowles was the master. She was lying in the river Thames. Mr. Stewart asked Captain Knowles to keep the slave on board till he set sail and then to be taken with him to Jamaica and there sold as a slave. Captain Knowles had him in irons in his ship. The slave then brought his writ of habeas corpus before Lord Mansfield — our great writ which guarantees a person freedom.

Mr. Stewart relied on the opinion of Lord Hardwicke and Lord Talbot in 1749. He also contended that in English law there was a precedent in the concept of 'villeinage' in the feudal system. (A 'villein' was a serf to his lord. The word survives now in our common word 'villain'.) Lord Mansfield rejected the argument in his eloquent passage (20 State Trials 1–82 and *Somerset v Stewart* (1772) Lofft 1–19):

'What ground is there for saying that the status of slavery is now recognised by the law of England? That trover will lie for a slave? That a slave-market may be established in Smithfield? I care not for the supposed dicta of judges, however eminent, if they be contrary to all principle. Villeinage, when it did exist in this country, differed in many particulars from West India slavery. The lord never could have thrown the villein into chains, sent him to the West Indies, and sold him there to work in a mine or in a cane field. At any rate, villeinage has ceased in England and it cannot be revived. Every man who comes into England is entitled to the protection of English law, whatever oppression he may heretofore have suffered and whatever may be the colour of his skin. The air of England is too pure for any slave to breathe. Let the black go free'.

That case preceded by nearly 200 years the Universal Declaration of Human Rights that:

'No one shall be held in slavery or servitude. Slavery and the slave trade shall be prohibited in all its forms'.

James Somerset came from a Crown Colony. The common law gave freedom to any alien who came into England from any country overseas. In the 18th century there were no customs officers, no passports to be presented at the ports. As soon as an alien set foot here, he was free. The extent of this freedom has since been limited by Statutes and Regulations. There are extradition treaties, immigration laws and deportation laws. But the scope of the common law fell to be considered in a spectacular case which came before our Court in 1963.

2 The fugitive from the United States

Dr. Soblen was a doctor of medicine. He was born in Lithuania (next to Russia) and practised there until he went to the United States in 1941. That was during the war. Whether he was a spy for the Russians we shall never know. All we

159

do know is that during the notorious 'McCarthy' purge in 1961 against communists he was charged with conspiring in 1944 and 1945 to give secrets to Russians. He was tried and convicted and sentenced to imprisonment for life. He appealed to the Supreme Court of the United States. He was allowed out on bail pending his appeal. His appeal was dismissed but on that very day, 25 June 1962, he broke his bail. He flew off to Israel, using his brother's passport. Israel refused to admit him. On 1 July 1962 they sent him back to the United States. They put him on an aircraft which was due to stop for a short while at London airport. About 20 miles out of London he severely wounded himself with a knife. He made a long cut on his wrist and he cut open his abdomen, ripping through the skin and the belly muscles. When the aircraft landed, it was essential, in order to save his life, that he should be removed at once to hospital. He was given blood transfusions. Six days later he was recovered sufficiently to be taken on to New York. But before that could happen, he applied for a writ of habeas corpus, claiming his freedom and that his detention was unjustified. He wanted to go to Czechoslovakia (next to Russia) but the United States Government wanted him to be sent there. Now his offence was not an extraditable offence. So he could not be extradited to the United States. In order to do what the United States wanted, the Home Secretary took another step. He made an order that Dr. Soblen be deported. That was the issue debated before the Court of Appeal. Was it lawful for the Home Secretary to order him to be deported? This is how we dealt with it in *R v Governor of Brixton Prison, ex parte Soblen*[1]:

'. . . . Although every alien, as soon as he lawfully sets foot in this country, is free, nevertheless the Crown is entitled at any time to send him home to his own country, if in its opinion his presence here is not conducive to the public good; and it may for this purpose arrest him and put him on board a ship or aircraft bound for his home country. That

1. [1963] 2 QB 243 at 300.

was clearly the law under the Aliens Order 1916 . . . and it is clear now under the Aliens Order of 1953. It is unnecessary to go into the state of the law before the Aliens Orders. I always understood that the Crown had a Royal Prerogative to expel an alien and send him home whenever it considered that his presence here was not conducive to the public good. Sir William Blackstone certainly said in his *Commentaries* – (1765), vol. 1, pages 259–260: "Strangers who come spontaneously" are "liable to be sent home whenever the King sees occasion". And this view is in accord with international law as stated by the law officers of the Crown (Sir Richard Webster. A-G, and Sir Robert Finlay, S-G) in 1896 in *Thomas Mann's* case[1]. It seems clear from that case that by international law any country is entitled to expel an alien if his presence is for any reason obnoxious to it; and as incidental to this right, it can arrest him, detain him, and put him on board a ship bound for his own country.

'I know that Professor Dicey said that the Crown has no means of arresting even the most dangerous aliens or of expelling them from the country (*Law of the Constitution* (1958 10th edn, page 224), and Professor Oppenheim (*International Law* (1955 8th edn, vol. 1, page 697) said the same. I am not at all sure that I agree with them. The matter was never tested in the courts. But it is not necessary to go into it now; for it is quite plain that the Royal Prerogative in this matter is now supplanted and replaced by the Aliens Order 1953 (articles 20 and 21), under which there is power in the Crown to deport an alien "if the Secretary of State deems it to be conducive to the public good": and for this purpose to detain him, and place him "on board any ship or aircraft which is about to leave the United Kingdom". Those words make it clear that the Home Secretary may choose the ship or aircraft and thus his destination.

'It was suggested before us that there was a common law shackle on this power of deportation. It was said that a man could not be deported, even to his own country, if he was a

---

1. Unreported (recorded in Lord McNair's *International Law Opinions* (1956), vol. 2, p. 111; see Tom Mann *Memoirs* (1923), pp. 135–138).

criminal who had fled from it. No authority was cited for this proposition. It cannot stand examination for one moment. Supposing no other country but his own is willing to take him. Are we to keep him here against our will simply because he is in his country a wanted man? Clearly not. If a fugitive criminal is here and the Secretary of State thinks that in the public good he ought to be deported, there is no reason why he should not be deported to his own country, even though he is there a wanted criminal. The Supreme Court of India considered this very point in 1955 in *Muller v Superintendent, Presidency Jail, Calcutta*[1], and in an instructive judgment made it quite clear that in their opinion the right to expel an alien could be exercised, even though he was wanted by his own country for a criminal offence. Even though his home country has requested that he should be sent back to them, I see no reason why the Home Secretary should not still deport him there, if his presence here is not conducive to the public good. The power to deport is not taken away by the fact that he is a fugitive from the justice of his own country, or by the fact that his own country wants him back and has made a request for him.

. . . .

'If, therefore, the purpose of the Home Secretary in this case was to surrender the applicant as a fugitive criminal to the United States of America because they had asked for him, then it would be unlawful. But if the Home Secretary's purpose was to deport him to his own country because the Home Secretary considered his presence here to be not conducive to the public good, then the Home Secretary's action is lawful. It is open to these courts to inquire whether the purpose of the Home Secretary was a lawful or an unlawful purpose. Was there a misuse of the power or not? The courts can always go behind the face of the deportation order in order to see whether the powers entrusted by Parliament have been exercised lawfully or no. . . .

'Then how does it rest in this case? The court cannot compel the Home Secretary to disclose the materials on

1. [1955] Int LR 497, (1955) SCJ 324.

which he acted, but if there is evidence on which it could reasonably be supposed that the Home Secretary was using the power of deportation for an ulterior purpose, then the court can call on the Home Secretary for an answer: and if he fails to give it, it can upset his order. But on the facts of this case I can find no such evidence. It seems to me that there was reasonable ground on which the Home Secretary could consider that the applicant's presence here was not conducive to the public good'.

So the order for deportation stood. All arrangements were made for Dr. Soblen to be put on an aircraft for the United States: with a US marshal to accompany him. But he avoided it all. Just before the day came, he took an overdose of drugs. He died here without recovering consciousness. Only his ashes were deported.

3 The student of 'Scientology'

One of the most important issues of the day is whether an alien (not a Commonwealth citizen) should be admitted into this country. The general law on the subject came up for consideration in a case about scientologists. 'Scientology' is an invented name. It finds no place in the English dictionaries. Its proponents say that scientology is a religion: and that this religion, its faith and belief, its teaching and practices, are taught to students at a college here in East Grinstead in Sussex. The number of students there was over 200 of whom approximately 100 were aliens. Two of them, Andrew Schmidt and Joseph Murranti, were citizens of the United States. They had permits for a limited time. The time expired. They wished to complete their studies and asked the Home Secretary to extend their permits. He refused. They brought an action against the Home Secretary saying that his refusal was invalid, because he did it for an unauthorised purpose. The Home Secretary applied to strike the action out. We did strike it out but only by a majority. It is reported as *Schmidt v Secretary of State for Home Affairs*[1]. I there stated the law in this way (page 168):

'The first point is whether there is any case for saying that the Home Secretary acted unlawfully in refusing an extension. Both sides accepted as correct the statement in *R v Governor of Brixton Prison, ex parte Soblen*[2], where I said that the validity of the Minister's act
"depends on the purpose with which the act is done. If it was done for an authorised purpose, it was lawful. If it was done professedly for an authorised purpose, but in fact for a different purpose with an ulterior object, it was unlawful".

'So I turn to consider what are the authorised purposes of the Home Secretary in respect of an alien — a friendly alien, no doubt — coming to this country. I have always held the view that at common law no alien has any right to enter this country except by leave of the Crown: and the Crown can refuse leave without giving any reason. The common law has now been overtaken by the Aliens Acts and the Orders thereunder.

. . . .

'The order thus gives to the Secretary of State ample power either to refuse admission to an alien or to grant him leave to enter for a limited period, or to refuse to extend his stay. Mr. Quintin Hogg sought to limit that power. He said that the Home Secretary could only have regard to three purposes: (1) the safety of the realm; (2) the observance of the law of the land; and (3) the preservation of the standards of morality generally accepted in this country. In the present case Mr. Hogg said that the Home Secretary did not exercise his power for any of those three authorised purposes, but for an unauthorised purpose which he stated to us in this way: The Home Secretary was, he said, using his power for the purpose of expressing disapproval of, and to bring into disrespect, a religious sect which was not prohibited by the law of the land. I do not think that the

1. [1969] 2 Ch 149.
2. [1963] 2 QB 243 at 302.

authorised purposes are limited in the way suggested by Mr. Hogg. I think the Minister can exercise his power for any purpose which he considers to be for the public good or to be in the interests of the people of this country. There is not the slightest ground for thinking that the Minister exercised his power here for any unauthorised purpose or with any ulterior motive. The Minister's purpose was clearly disclosed in the statement which was made to the House of Commons. He thought that the practices of these people, these scientologists, were most harmful to our society, and that it was undesirable in the interests of the people of this country that alien students of scientology should be allowed to stay any longer or that any new ones should be allowed to come in. That purpose was entirely justifiable. It was exercised by the Home Secretary in the interests of the ordinary people of this country: and I do not think we should admit any doubt to be thrown on its validity'.

4 Freedom of movement

Now there is an interesting sequel to that case. It arose out of the adherence of this Court to the European Economic Community. How far are the principles of *Schmidt's* case applicable now that we have joined the Common Market? There is a clause in the Treaty of Rome which guarantees freedom of movement to workers within the Community. This means that a worker in any one of the nine countries is entitled as of right to move to any other country of the nine so as to get work, or to study. But there is an exception (strangely worded) where there are reasons of public policy for restricting this freedom. Now Miss Van Duyn was a Dutch girl. She arrived at Gatwick airport and declared that she had come to take up employment as a secretary at the College of Scientology at East Grinstead. The immigration officer refused her permission on the ground that it was undesirable to give anyone leave to enter the United Kingdom to be in the employment of the Church of Scientology. She challenged that refusal. She claimed that under Article 48 of the Treaty of Rome (which is part of our law) she was entitled to enter England under the basic community right of 'freedom of movement'. The point was referred to the European Court of Justice at Luxembourg. It was the first case ever referred to that Court from England. Their decision is reported in *Van Duyn v Home Office*[1]. It seemed to me then, and it seems to me now, that Miss Van Duyn had a very good case under the Treaty. She was a girl of excellent character. If she had been an English girl living in England, she could have taken up employment at East Grinstead with the College of Scientology — without any let or hindrance whatever. Why should Miss Van Duyn be denied freedom — now that there is free movement for workers? There was in her favour a directive which said that, if she was to be refused entry on grounds of public policy, it had to be 'based exclusively on the personal conduct of the individual concerned'. The European Court held that this 'personal conduct' included the fact that she was 'associated with some body or organisation the activities of which the member state considers socially harmful'. So Miss Van Duyn could be excluded because she intended to go to the College of Scientology. It is a good illustration of the way in which the European Court interprets the Treaty and the Directives. It is taking policy considerations into account.

1. [1975] Ch 358.

2 Commonwealth citizens

Introduction

About 20 years ago the people of England began to be worried about the influx of citizens coming from the British Commonwealth: that is, those who came from the great Dominions and Colonies which in the past formed part of the British Empire.

Before 1962 any Commonwealth citizen could come as of right into this country without the leave of anyone. He could stay here as long as he liked. He had the same rights as any native-born Englishman. He could not be detained by the executive without a trial. If he committed a crime, he was liable to be arrested and tried like anyone else. But he could not be deported, not even if he was a habitual criminal, nor even if his presence here was obnoxious to the rest of the people.

By a series of Acts and Rules these rights have been taken away. I will not go into the details except to say that the law has been revolutionised by the Immigration Act 1971. Commonwealth citizens are now to be divided into two classes: First, *patrials* – these have the right of abode here and can come and go without let or hindrance. Secondly, *non-patrials* – these have no right to come here or to remain here except by leave. That leave is given by the Home Secretary acting through the immigration officer. If they enter here without leave they are 'illegal entrants'. Much of the details of the law is now contained in Immigration Rules issued by the Home Secretary under the authority of the

Statute. But there are some leading cases on the subject to which I would draw your attention.

1 'Patrials'

'Patrial' is a word used to describe a Commonwealth citizen who has settled here lawfully for five years or more. He then acquires a 'right of abode' here. I ventured to describe it in the important case of *R v Home Secretary, ex parte Phansopkar*[1]:

'In 1971 the Parliament of the United Kingdom invented a new word. It made a new man. It called him "patrial". Not a patriot, but a patrial. Parliament made him one of us: and made us one of them. We are all now patrials. We are no longer, in the eye of the law, Englishmen, Scotsmen or Welshmen. We are just patrials. Parliament gave this new man a fine set of clothes. It invested him with a new right. It called it "the right of abode in the United Kingdom". It is the most precious right that anyone can have. At least I so regard it. It is declared in simple but expressive words. Every patrial "shall be free to live in, and to come and go into and from, the United Kingdom without let or hindrance"; section 1(1) of the Immigration Act 1971.

'At the same time, Parliament made it very easy for many an immigrant to become a patrial and get this precious right. Those of us who were born here and live here get it automatically. Those coming from overseas get it by being registered as "a citizen of the United Kingdom and Colonies". This is not difficult, at any rate, not for anyone who has been living here for five years, provided that he is a Commonwealth citizen. If he comes, for instance, from Canada or Australia or, I must add, India or Bangladesh, and is of good character and has a sufficient knowledge of English he can become registered as a "citizen of the United Kingdom and Colonies". And here is the important point. Not only does he himself, on registration, become a patrial and entitled to

1. [1976] QB 606 at 615.

the right of abode here, but also his wife does automatically. Even though she is living in far-off India or Bangladesh. Even though she has never been to England and cannot speak a word of English. She, too, becomes a patrial and entitled to the right of abode here. So she has the right to come into the United Kingdom without let or hindrance: bringing, no doubt, her babies with her. The only thing in her way is that she has to prove that she is his wife or, I suppose, one of his wives, if by their law, such is permitted. To prove this, she has to get a "certificate of patriality". She can get this in her homeland by going to the British High Commission and satisfying the officers there that her husband is a patrial and that she is his wife. But there is a very long queue there of people wanting to get entry clearance for England. It may take 18 months or more to get an interview with the officer. Some of these husbands and wives are upset by this waiting in the queue. Three or four wives have tried to jump the queue. They have come to England without getting a certificate of patriality beforehand. Soon after arriving at Heathrow they have applied for a certificate here. The Home Office have refused, saying: "We are not going to consider your application here. It would be much more satisfactorily dealt with in Bombay or Dacca. So back you go. You cannot be allowed to jump the queue. It would not be fair to the others who have lined up in it". This reply has been challenged by the people here who are advising immigrants on their rights. They rely amongst other things on the European Convention for the Protection of Human Rights and Fundamental Freedoms, to which we have adhered. It gives in Article 8 the right to respect for family life and says that there shall be no interference with it, except such as is in accordance with the law and is necessary in a democratic society'.

Then I set out the facts. I described how Mr. Phansopkar came from India to England in 1966, lived here and worked here for several years, and then in 1974 obtained a certificate by which he was registered as a citizen of the United

Kingdom and Colonies. Similarly, how Mr. Rouf came from
East Pakistan (now Bangladesh) in 1960 and obtained a
certificate of citizenship on 16 March 1962. I continued
(page 617):

'. . . . Having obtained that certificate, the husband became
entitled to a most valuable right. He himself thenceforward
has "the right of abode in the United Kingdom". His right
was equal to the right of abode of any of us. You and I and
our families have been born here and lived here from time
immemorial. Yet Mr. Phansopkar, from the moment he was
registered, had just as much right here as we have. He became
a citizen of no mean country. He could say proudly, if he
spoke Latin — *civis angliae sum.* He became a patrial.

'And not only he. His wife also obtained at that very
moment the self-same right. She had never been to England.
She could not speak English. She could not read or write. She
lived in India with her four young children. But she was a
Commonwealth citizen. And, as such, as soon as her husband,
by registration, gained the right of abode in the United
Kingdom, she acquired the self-same right of abode: see
section 2(2) of the Immigration Act 1971. This right was
conferred on her husband and on her by section 1(1) of the
Act of 1971 in these wide and generous terms:
"All those who are in this Act expressed to have the right of
abode in the United Kingdom shall be free to live in, and to
come and go into and from, the United Kingdom without let
or hindrance"'.

Then we decided in favour of the wife in these words (page
621):

'Each of these two ladies is entitled to come into England
without let or hindrance provided that she is truly the wife
of her husband. She does not have to seek permission. She
comes as of right and not by leave. No one can refuse to
admit her, provided she can prove it by means of a certificate
of patriality: section 3(9) of the Act of 1971.

'Such being her right, I do not think it can be taken away
by arbitrarily refusing her a certificate, or by delaying to

issue it to her without good cause. She can invoke Magna Carta: "To none will we sell: to no one will we delay or deny right or justice". It seems to me to be implicit in this legislation that a wife, who is truly a wife, is entitled to apply for a certificate of patriality and to have her application examined fairly and in a reasonable time. . . .

. . . .

'The only remedy for each of the ladies is an order in the nature of mandamus. In the special circumstances of these cases, I think the order should issue. The Home Secretary ought not to send these ladies back to India and Bangladesh to face long delays. He ought to examine the applications to see whether or not each lady is a patrial and to give or refuse a certificate according to whether she satisfies him, or not. I would allow the appeal, accordingly'.

2 'Illegal entrants'

Next there are those who come into this country clandestinely, in breach of our immigration laws. They are 'illegal entrants'. A typical case was Gurbax Singh Khera. He was born in a village in the Punjab. He had an uncle in the same village. His uncle arranged with agents in India to get him to England – on payment of 15,000 rupees. He travelled by air from New Delhi to Paris. Then by car to a port on the French coast. When it was dark he embarked on a small motor-boat with three other Asians. The boat was manned by two white men. He was frightened because it was his first time at sea. They crossed to England. They got out on a sandy shore. The white men led them to hard ground. The Asians were put in the back of a van. They were driven for five or six hours till they arrived at Wolverhampton. He was dropped at his father's house. He soon obtained work and has continued at work ever since. Some years later he was arrested and detained as an 'illegal entrant'. He applied for a writ of habeas corpus. His was one of three cases which were considered by the Court of Appeal and the House of Lords, reported as

171

R v Governor of Pentonville Prison, ex parte Azam[1]. This is what I said (page 24):

'These three cases raise questions of the first importance to many Commonwealth citizens now in this country. Each of the three men is an "illegal entrant". Each entered this country clandestinely without any permission to do so. Each has worked here for more than three years. Each has now been arrested and detained in prison. In each case without trial. Each is about to be removed under the directions of the Home Secretary from this country. Each has brought a writ of habeas corpus claiming that his detention is unlawful.

'Other cases await our decision. There must be many "illegal entrants" wondering whether it will be their turn next. No one can tell the number. They came in secretly. They went to ground for a time. Afterwards they mingled with others. They got lost in the crowd. Frequently they have managed to get passports of some kind. They go to their High Commissioners and say that they did have passports which have been lost or damaged. On that plea they have been issued with new ones. There is no easy way of telling a legal from an illegal entrant. They have obtained work. They have been issued with National Insurance cards. Now, under the new Act which came into force on 1 January 1973 they are faced with arrest and removal. The situation is shown by the facts in these three cases'.

I then set out the facts and said (page 33):

'In setting out the facts relating to these three men, I have done so with some sympathy for them. Coming from a Commonwealth country, where there is desperate poverty, they sought refuge in this country – a country where they can obtain work at good wages; where there are social services beyond compare; and where, above all, the law still protects the freedom of the individual. No doubt they had heard of friends and relatives who had come and settled here, and done well. No doubt there were grasping agents

1. [1974] AC 18.

ready to take their money to arrange a passage. Yet they must have known that their entry was unlawful. No one enters a country by night in a small boat if he is coming in lawfully. They must have known that there was a queue of people waiting to come in lawfully: and that they were jumping the queue. They must have known, too, that their stay here was precarious. So they did all they could to get passports of seeming validity. No doubt they hoped all the time that they would not be found out. To be fair to them, they seem to have behaved well and worked well. After three years, some might think that their wrongdoing could be forgiven, and that there should be an amnesty. But Parliament has decided otherwise. I think I can see why. These men, if once here by leave, will seek to bring their wives and children over. Two of them have already applied to do so. If the men are allowed to remain, it will be difficult to refuse the wives and children. If this were allowed, the number of immigrants would be increased so greatly that there would not be room for everybody. Again, if an amnesty were granted, it would be an encouragement to others to follow their example: and that simply cannot be permitted. By sending back illegal entrants, it will help to deter others from trying to do the same.

'In the circumstances Parliament, as I read the Act, has decided that illegal entrants can be sent back. It has entrusted this decision to the Home Secretary, and not to the courts. It has left it to his discretion. It is better left there because, after all, the matter is one of policy which the courts cannot handle. The Home Secretary can take into account all the circumstances. He has to weigh in the balance on the one hand the length of time the man has been here, and his conduct while here: and, on the other hand, the effect on our society if he and others like him are allowed to stay. This is not a justiciable matter for the courts. It is an administrative matter for the Secretary of State. It is very like his discretion to remove aliens, which has never been questioned in all our long history. Illegal entrants cannot expect to be treated better than aliens. Even though they are Commonwealth citizens, they have come into this country in flagrant defiance of our laws. They cannot pray in aid those very laws so as to enable them to remain here. The invasion by them has reached such a scale that Parliament has said: "This must be stopped. The Home Secretary can send them back". If he orders their removal, the courts cannot interfere with his decision. But I would emphasise that this power of the Home Secretary can only be exercised when the man is in truth an illegal entrant. It is very different from the power given in war-time under regulation 18B. Under that regulation a man could be detained on suspicion — suspicion that he was of hostile association. Here he can only be removed if he was in truth guilty — guilty of having unlawfully entered. Under regulation 18B it was dependent on the opinion of the Home Secretary — if he had reasonable cause to believe. Here it is dependent on matter of fact — whether he was an illegal entrant. Under regulation 18B the decision could hardly ever be challenged by habeas corpus. Here it can be. The Home Secretary can, if called upon, be required to show that the man was an illegal entrant. With these safeguards, none of these men can justly complain if the Home Secretary should decide that he shall be removed. I would, therefore, dismiss these appeals'.

That case was decided by the Court of Appeal on 3 May 1973 and affirmed by the House of Lords a month later on 11 June 1973. You will notice there that I spoke of an amnesty. This was granted — not by any Statute — but by a statement by the Home Secretary in the House of Commons. He announced on 11 April 1974 that he would not use the power of removal under the Immigration Act 1971 to send away Commonwealth citizens who entered the United Kingdom illegally before 1 January 1973.

That amnesty did not apply to those who entered illegally after 1 January 1973. We have had cases since where some came clandestinely *after* 1 January 1973 but sought to say they came *before* that date. Those cases depended on their facts. The immigration officers always inquired into the circumstances very fairly. If they came in after 1 January 1973 they were sent back whence they came.

3 'Expelled' persons

In 1972 a sword fell on the Asians living in Uganda. It was
the sword of the President, General Amin. He declared that
all Asians who were not citizens of Uganda must leave the
country within 90 days. The declaration placed thousands in
sore plight. Those who had British passports came to England
and were admitted here. But some had not. One of them was
Pravinlal Thakrar. He went to Austria for a year and then
came by air to London. He told the immigration officer that
he had come to England and that he had a right to be here.
He was detained pending further inquiries. Then he applied
for certiorari and mandamus. The case is reported as *R v
Immigration Officer, ex parte Thakrar*[1]. He was represented
by Sir Dingle Foot QC, the most experienced of all in matters
relating to the countries of the Commonwealth – past or
present – and the most expert. He submitted that Thakrar
had a right to enter England: because he was a British protected person. This is how we dealt with it (page 701):

'Sir Dingle Foot, on behalf of Pravinlal, raises this fundamental point: let us assume for the time being that Pravinlal
is, as he asserts, a British protected person. Sir Dingle says
that as such he is a British national just as much as a citizen
of the United Kingdom and Colonies. As a British national, if
he is expelled from the land where he is living, he is entitled
as of right to come into the United Kingdom. This right, says
Sir Dingle, is given by international law: and international
law, he says, is part of the law of the land. It is incorporated
into it and is to be enforced by the courts unless it is
excluded by Parliament. To support this claim in international
law, Sir Dingle Foot quoted *Oppenheim's International Law*,
8th ed. (1955), vol. 1, pages 645–646: "The home state of
expelled persons is bound to receive them on the home
territory".

'To support his assertion that international law is part of
the law of the land, Sir Dingle quoted Sir William Blackstone
in his *Commentaries*, 17th ed. (1830), Book IV, page 67, and

1. [1974] QB 684.

Lord Mansfield in *Heathfield v Chilton* (1767) 4 Burr 2016.
They said that the law of nations is "part of the law of the
land". . . .

'Test it by reference to the very point we have to consider
here: the mass expulsion of Asians from Uganda. International law has never had to cope with such a problem. None
of the jurists, so far as I can discover, has considered it. The
statement in *Oppenheim* is all very well when one is considering a home state which is a *self-contained* country with no
overseas territories or protectorates. If one of its citizens goes
to a foreign country and is expelled from it, the home state
may well be bound to accept him on his home territory if he
has nowhere else to go. But that rule does not apply when
the home state is an outgoing country with far-flung commit-
ments abroad, such as the United Kingdom has or recently
did have. Take the class of persons with whom we are here
concerned — British protected persons. They are said to be
British nationals, but they are not British subjects. These
number, or used to number, many millions. They were not
born here. They have never lived here. They live thousands
of miles away in countries which have no connection with
England except that they were once British protectorates. Is
it to be said that by international law every one of them has
a right if expelled to come into these small islands? Surely
not. This country would not have room for them. It is not as
if it was only one or two coming. They come not in single
files "but in battalions". Mass expulsions have never hitherto
come within the cognisance of international law. To my
mind, there is no rule of international law to which we may
have recourse. There is no rule by which we are bound to
receive them'.

I continued with these words (page 707):

'. . . . Pravinlal Thakrar has asserted that he is a British protected person, and that, on being expelled from Uganda, he
has a legal right to enter this country. I am satisfied that he
has no such right. There is no legal right in him to enter this
country. If he had been a British protected person, that would

be a factor in his favour which would be given serious consideration by the immigration officers and by the Secretary of
State. It might tip the scale and he might be allowed to enter.
But Pravinlal never got anywhere near showing that he was
a British protected person. So he is not entitled to any special
consideration. Everyone will be sorry for the plight in which
he finds himself. He is a man of standing, intelligence and
ability. But he ought to consider this: his father and mother
are in India. His wife and two children are in India. It might
be better for him to join them in that great country, where
there may be more scope for him than here. This country is
not large enough to take in all those whom we would gladly
accept. . .'.

Such is the law but the Home Secretary has a dispensing
power. He exercises it generously in the interests of humanity.
Many of those expelled from Uganda were brought here,
housed and fed, found work and settled here. So far as I
know, they were appreciative and none had any complaints.

4 Overstayers and others

Such are the leading cases when non-patrials sought to
enter or to stay without leave. But many came in as visitors
with leave for a month or more: or as students with leave
for a year or more. A great number of these, having
obtained leave, went underground. They overstayed their
leave. They were lost without trace. Sometimes they were
discovered – by some chance or other – and then detained.
Sometimes they were allowed to remain on compassionate
grounds. In other cases the Home Secretary made a deportation order. They were given the benefit of an appeal procedure – to an adjudicator – and thence to the Immigration
Appeal Tribunal. The statutory provisions were so complex
that one reached the Court of Appeal – *R v Immigration
Tribunal, ex parte Subramaniam*[1] and another the House of
Lords – *Suthendrian v Immigration Appeal Tribunal*[2] where

1. [1977] QB 190.
2. [1977] AC 359.

there was a division of opinion 3 to 2. But these are so complicated that I would not trouble you to read them. Suffice it to say that the amnesty did not apply to these overstayers. If they overstayed before 1973 they were still liable to deportation.

Another large group of cases was where a person comes in by air and gets through the immigration control by presenting forged papers to the immigration officer: or making false statements to him. Afterwards the fraud is discovered. He is detained: and a deportation order is made. Again the amnesty does not apply to them. In all these cases where a person is not a patrial — and can only enter or remain by leave — the Home Secretary has, by the authority of section 3(2) of the Statute made rules as to the practice to be followed by immigration officers: These rules deal with control *on entry*, control *after entry*, both as to Commonwealth citizens and as to non-Commonwealth nationals. The rules are so comprehensive that the officers have only to see whether the applicants come within them or not, likewise the Appeal Tribunals. So they are not appropriate for treatment here. Suffice it to say that in the many cases reaching the High Court, it seems to me that the immigration officers do their work efficiently and honestly and fairly. I have never known a case where they have been unfair.

3 Exits

Introduction

The law has placed no restriction on people going out from England to avoid tax or for any other reason. There was in olden days a writ called *ne exeat regnum*. Sir William Blackstone in his *Commentaries* (I.137) said that:

'The King, indeed, by his royal prerogative, may issue out his writ *ne exeat regnum* and prohibit any of his subjects from going into foreign parts without licence. This may be necessary for the public service and safeguard of the Commonwealth'.

And Lord Campbell in his *Lives of the Lord Chancellors* (I.13) said:

'The Chancellor has an exclusive authority to restrain a party from leaving the kingdom, where it appears that he is purposely withdrawing himself from the jurisdiction of the court, to the disappointment of honest creditors. This is effected by the writ *ne exeat regno*, issuing under the great seal; – a high prerogative remedy, which, as it affects personal liberty, is granted with great circumspection, particularly where foreigners are concerned'.

I must say that I have never known a case in modern times where this writ has been issued: and I should think it is now obsolete. Especially now that imprisonment for debt has been abolished. A creditor has now a better remedy by way of a *Mareva* injunction, which does not trespass upon personal liberty.

But the law still does what it can to discourage citizens taking unfair advantage of their liberty to go abroad.

1 A move to Jersey

As everyone knows, Jersey is a favourite haven for the tax avoider. Mr. Stanley Weston is typical. He was born in Russia and came to England when he was 18. He made a fortune here. He made settlements in favour of his children of shares in his company. In the case, *Re Weston's Settlements*[1], I said:

'When those settlements were entered into, there was no capital gains tax. But in the next year, 1965, Parliament imposed the capital gains tax which is payable on capital gains accruing to persons resident in the United Kingdom. The tax is at the rate of 30 per cent. The result was that if the trustees and beneficiaries remained here and the shares of Stanley Weston increased in value (as they have), there would sooner or later be a heavy liability to capital gains tax. This was such an uncomfortable prospect that Mr. Stanley Weston took steps to remove his family to the Channel Islands, and the trusts as well'.

They all went, Mr. Weston, his wife and children, to Jersey and set up house there. Three months later he applied to the Chancery Division to sanction the removal of the settlements to Jersey. It was said that this would be greatly to the financial advantage of the young children and unborn children. We declined to sanction the removal. I said (at page 245):

'. . . . There are many things in life more worth-while than money. One of these things is to be brought up in this our England, which is still "the envy of less happier lands". I do not believe it is for the benefit of children to be uprooted from England and transported to another country simply to avoid tax. It was very different with the children of the Seale family, which Buckley J considered. That family had

1. [1969] 1 Ch 223 at 242.

emigrated to Canada many years before, with no thought of tax avoidance, and had brought up the children there as Canadians. It was very proper that the trust should be transferred to Canada. But here the family had only been in Jersey three months when they presented this scheme to the court. The inference is irresistible: the underlying purpose was to go there in order to avoid tax. I do not think that this will be all to the good for the children. I should imagine that, even if they had stayed in this country, they would have had a very considerable fortune at their disposal, even after paying tax. The only thing that Jersey can do for them is to give them an even greater fortune. Many a child has been ruined by being given too much. The avoidance of tax may be lawful, but it is not yet a virtue. The Court of Chancery should not encourage or support it – it should not give its approval to it – if by so doing it would imperil the true welfare of the children, already born or yet to be born.

'There is one thing more. I cannot help wondering how long these young people will stay in Jersey. It may be to their financial interest at present to make their home there permanently. But will they remain there once the capital gains are safely in hand, clear of tax? They may well change their minds and come back to enjoy their untaxed gains. Is such a prospect really for the benefit of the children? Are they to be wanderers over the face of the earth, moving from this country to that, according to where they can best avoid tax? I cannot believe that to be right. Children are like trees: they grow stronger with firm roots.

'The long and short of it is, as the judge said, that the exodus of this family to Jersey is done to avoid British taxation. Having made great wealth here, they want to quit without paying the taxes and duties which are imposed on those who stay. So be it. If it really be for the benefit of the children, let it be done. Let them go, taking their money with them. But, if it be not truly for their benefit, the court should not countenance it. It should not give the scheme its blessing. The judge refused his approval. So would I. I would dismiss this appeal'.

We have just been to Jersey for the Annual Conference of the Law Society. So delightful that I no longer think ill of the tax avoiders.

2 Dr Wallersteiner, I presume

Now I turn to those who operate companies registered abroad in tax-havens. I start with one of the most elusive figures who has ever been concerned in our Courts. It is Dr. Wallersteiner. The case about him is *Wallersteiner v Moir*[1]. He was a scientist turned financier. He was of German origin but came to England. He did well. He had an office in the City of London and a residence in the West End. He controlled many concerns, in England and abroad. Some of them were registered in Liechtenstein. That is a tiny European state between Switzerland and Austria with a population of 20,000 all told. His concerns carried on no business in Liechtenstein at all. He had other concerns elsewhere. A very useful one was registered in the Bahamas, another in Nigeria, and so forth. He sought to avoid his liabilities by saying that his transactions were those of those companies and not his. This is how we dealt with it (page 1013):

'It is plain that Dr. Wallersteiner used many companies, trusts, or other legal entities as if they belonged to him. He was in control of them as much as any "one-man company" is under the control of the one man who owns all the shares and is the chairman and managing director. He made contracts of enormous magnitude on their behalf on a sheet of notepaper without reference to anyone else. . . .

'Mr. Browne-Wilkinson, as amicus curiae, suggested that all these various concerns were used by Dr. Wallersteiner as a façade: so that each could be treated as his alter ego. Each was in reality Dr. Wallersteiner wearing another hat.

'Mr. Anthony Lincoln, for Dr. Wallersteiner, repudiated this suggestion. It was quite wrong, he said, to pierce the corporate veil. The principle enunciated in *Salomon v*

1. [1974] 1 WLR 991.

182

Salomon & Co Ltd[1] was sacrosanct. If we were to treat each of these concerns as being Dr. Wallersteiner himself under another hat, we should not, he said, be lifting a corner of the corporate veil. We should be sending it up in flames.

'I am prepared to accept that the English concerns — those governed by English company law or its counterparts in Nassau or Nigeria — were distinct legal entities. I am not so sure about the Liechtenstein concerns — such as the Rothschild Trust, the Cellpa Trust or Stawa AG. There was no evidence before us of Liechtenstein law. I will assume, too, that they were distinct legal entities, similar to an English limited company. Even so, I am quite clear that they were just the puppets of Dr. Wallersteiner. He controlled their every movement. Each danced to his bidding. He pulled the strings. No one else got within reach of them. Transformed into legal language, they were his agents to do as he commanded. He was the principal behind them. I am of the opinion that the court should pull aside the corporate veil and treat these concerns as being his creatures — for whose doings he should be, and is, responsible. At any rate, it was up to him to show that any one else had a say in their affairs and he never did so: . . .'.

3 The giant chartering group

Very recently a giant chartering group failed to meet its liabilities. It had funds in a bank in London. The creditors sought a *Mareva* injunction to restrain it from disposing of the London funds. The chartering group asserted that it had huge assets and ought not to be subjected to a *Mareva* injunction. But it appeared that it was a company registered in Panama. It carried on no business in Panama. Its transactions were all 'offshore operations'. On these grounds we upheld the grant of a *Mareva* injunction. The case was *Third Chandris Corporation v Unimarine* where I said[2]:

1. [1897] AC 22.
2. [1979] 3 WLR 122 at 138.

'. . . . We often see in this court a corporation which is registered in a country where the company law is so loose that nothing is known about it — where it does no work and has no officers and no assets. Nothing can be found out about the membership, or its control, or its assets, or the charges on them. Judgment cannot be enforced against it. There is no reciprocal enforcement of judgments. It is nothing more than a name grasped from the air, as elusive as the Cheshire cat. In such cases the very fact of incorporation there gives some ground for believing there is a risk that, if judgment or an award is obtained, it may go unsatisfied. . .'.

Part six

Ventures into family law

1 How I learned the trade

1 I became a Divorce Judge

Before I became a judge, I never did a divorce case. Not that I had any religious objection. I am not a Roman Catholic. But divorce work was considered inferior and unpleasant. The best juniors did not touch it. No one in our chambers did any. The fashionable silks might now and again, if paid enough. But not us.

Yet, on my appointment to the Bench, I was assigned to the Divorce Division. It was strange how it happened. I was engaged as counsel in the House of Lords. It was on 6 March 1944, three months before D Day. The Lords were not sitting in their own Chamber. They were sitting in a room nearby. It was the King's (now the Queen's) Robing Room at the end of the Royal Gallery. The Chamber of the Commons had been destroyed by enemy action: and they sat in the Lords' Chamber. The Lords sat judicially in the mornings only. The Lord Chancellor, Viscount Simon, was presiding. It is a reported case, *Reville v Prudential Assurance Co Ltd*[1]. It was all about war damage. I was instructed by the Prudential Assurance Co. By that time I had very respectable clients. Moss Turner-Samuels was against me. He was a hardened warrior. He took every point, good or bad, usually bad. (His son David, a QC, now takes the good points.) At the end of my argument the Lord Chancellor asked me to come to his room. He said he would like me to be a judge: and if I agreed, he wished me to be appointed, in the first instance, to the Divorce Division. It was because of the wartime separations of husbands and wives: leading to a

1. [1944] AC 135.

great increase in divorce cases. I agreed. I have never refused any appointment requested by a Lord Chancellor of me. (Save when Lord Gardiner in 1968 asked me to return to the Lords.) On this occasion in 1944 the Lord Chancellor told me he wished to announce it at once, even though our case was not finished. So I was appointed a judge on 7 March 1944 whilst the case was still part-heard. The youngest judge (save for Lord Hodson) for 150 years. I was just 45. A widower. My wife had died just over two years earlier. My little son — then aged 5 — came with me when I was sworn in. Lord Simon showed him the Great Seal and asked him: 'Do you know which King threw it into the river Thames?' I could not have answered it myself. I know now that it was James II, who thought it was the source of all lawful authority. As he was rowed across the Thames in a small boat, he threw the Great Seal into the midst of the stream; after many months, it was accidentally caught by a fishing net and dragged up[1].

On the same day two others were appointed Judges of the Divorce Division. They were older than me. One was Hubert Wallington, an able common lawyer but a Roman Catholic quite unfitted for the Divorce Division. He allowed his beliefs to affect his decisions. The other was Harry Barnard, a respected practitioner in the Division. A solid good judge. He retired in 1959 as soon as he had done his 15 years. He has lived on his pension for the last 20 years and is now 88. I have gone on. It is because I like the work.

2 Sitting to try divorce cases

I sat in London during the first few months. Early in the war arrangements had been made for the Courts to be evacuated to Oxford; but we never left the Strand. I argued cases in the basement before Lord Greene, the Master of the Rolls. But when I was appointed a judge, it was the time of the flying bombs. On one occasion in the basement after lunch, two witnesses turned up to give evidence — their faces cut by splinters from the bombs. One morning I got to my room

1. Mac. ulay *History of England*, Ch. IX.

in the Courts and found the windows blasted and broken glass everywhere. At home back in Cuckfield we were in the flight path of enemy bombers. They dropped their unused bombs on to us. One afternoon we had a grandstand view of the first flying bomb shot down by a Spitfire. We carried on as usual of course. As Lord Atkin said in *Liversidge v Anderson*[1]:

'In this country, amid the clash of arms, the laws are not silent: they may be changed, but they speak the same language in war as in peace'.

I disliked the divorce work. It was sordid in the extreme. Everything depended on proof of a matrimonial offence — adultery, cruelty or desertion. Horrid details were the daily menu. In undefended cases the chambermaid would give evidence that, when she took up the early morning tea, the couple were there in bed. 'Was this the man?' asks counsel, showing a photograph of the husband. 'Yes, sir'. 'Was this the woman?', showing a photograph of the wife. 'No, sir'. In one contested case the husband said he had got infected with venereal disease from a lavatory seat. I did not believe him. In another, the wife denied there were stains on the sheet. I did not believe her. The sordidness was relieved when noble families were involved. Sir Patrick Hastings on one side, the most devastating cross-examiner ever. Gilbert Beyfus on the other — compelling by his choice of words and a strange twitch in his face.

3 Over to the King's Bench

Thank goodness I only did Divorce for 18 months. After the General Election, Lord Jowitt on 2 August 1945 became Lord Chancellor. I had often been his junior in big cases at the bar, such as *Beresford v Royal Insurance Co*[2]. He did not think I was in the right place. One of the very first things he did was to transfer me to the King's Bench Division. It was on 24 October 1945. I went at once on the Midland Circuit.

1. [1942] AC 206 at 244.
2. [1938] AC 586.

Amongst other places to Lincoln where my mother was born in the Bail Gate. My grandfather had served in the Crimean War of 1854–1856. He used to blow the trumpets when the Judges of Assize came to Lincoln. How proud he would have been when I came.

So ended my service as a Divorce Judge. I did not reserve a single judgment for a whole year. That is good advice for a new judge. But I was learning all the time. I was getting the feel of things. Sometimes I was reversed. My extempore judgment on 13 December 1944 on connivance was reversed by the Court of Appeal in *Churchman v Churchman*[1]. But when I gained confidence I started to put principles into writing. My first reserved judgment was, as it happened, about a matrimonial home. It was on 28 March 1945 and is reported in *Smith v Smith*[2]. Soon after I had to consider the ever-recurring subject of presumptions and burdens. It was on 6 July 1945 and is reported in *Emanuel v Emanuel*[3]. So much so that I wrote an article on it for *The Law Quarterly Review*. The editor, wise Arthur Goodhart, approved it but told me that I ought to have supported my principles by reference to more authorities. I added therefore a last paragraph. It is the issue of *The Law Quarterly Review* for October 1945:

'The reader will have noticed that the illustrations in this article are all taken from familiar cases, but I have not given the references to many of them. This is because I am concerned here, not with particular branches of law, but with a new set of distinctions running through the whole law, in an attempt to remove the confusion produced by the old'.

4 On circuit

Soon after my transfer to the King's Bench, I remarried. It was in December 1945. Widow and widower. We combined our two families. Then I exercised the privilege always

1. [1945] P 44.
2. (1945) 61 TLR 331.
3. [1946] P 115.

accorded to a new judge. I chose to go my own circuit, the Western. My wife drove in her old car DGP 745 (we called it 'Dogpie') with my son of 7 and step-daughter of 17. I do not drive. I always say: 'If anyone is to be convicted of careless driving, it is not this Judge'. All the way round the Western Circuit. Those lovely places — Salisbury, Dorchester, Wells, Bodmin and on to Exeter, 'the ever-faithful city'. There, on the first evening, the Colonel of the Depot came to the lodgings and asked the traditional question, dating back to the times when the troops were troublesome: 'My Lord, I come to ask if the men can be allowed out of barracks'. I replied with the traditional words: 'Are the troops all loyal?' He answered truly but not in tradition: 'Yes, all three of them'. The barracks were empty.

5 Chairmanship of the Divorce Committee

I had looked forward to going on to Bristol and Winchester. My mother was then still alive. But the Lord Chancellor, Lord Jowitt, called me back from Exeter. It was to chair a Committee on the administration of the law of Divorce[1]. In particular to recommend methods by which the existing delays in divorce proceedings might be eliminated. The Committee was a good one. It included Terence Donovan (afterwards Lord Donovan), Sir Edwin Herbert (afterwards Lord Tangley), and John Foster (afterwards Sir John Foster). He managed to listen to the evidence and write letters at the same time. Tom Skyrme (afterwards Sir Thomas Skyrme) was the Secretary. He was most efficient. We took no time off from Court. We sat in a committee room in the Lords from 4.30 p.m. to 7 p.m. We worked quickly. No Committee has ever worked so quickly or so well. We were appointed on 26 June 1946. By the end of July we presented an interim report[2] recommending that the period between decree nisi and decree absolute should be reduced from six months to

1. Committee on Procedure in Matrimonial Causes.
2. Cmnd. 6881.

six weeks. It was implemented at once. In a second interim report[1] in November 1946 we recommended that divorce cases should no longer be tried only by High Court judges. They should be tried by county court judges sitting as commissioners. It was implemented at once. In a final report[2] in February 1947 we recommended that there should be a Marriage Welfare Service to afford help and guidance both in preparation for marriage and also in difficulties after marriage. Further, that welfare officers should be appointed to the courts, especially to help about the children. Unusual for committees, all our recommendations were accepted and implemented. At the end we had a dinner to which the Lord Chancellor came. They presented me with the Report bound in handsome leather in which he wrote:

> 'To Mr. Justice Denning
> With all my thanks
> for the great work he has done.
> 23rd April 1947   Jowitt C'

But there was one who did not agree with the Report: and he was the most concerned of all. He was the President of the Divorce Division, Lord Merriman: and it would fall to him to implement most of the recommendations. He came and gave evidence before the Committee, but it was at an early stage before we had got very far: and I am sorry to say that we did not get his views on some of the most important recommendations. In particular, on the recommendation that there should be welfare officers attached to the Court. It certainly was a mistake on our part not to see him again. He felt very strongly about this. He never forgave me. When I happened to go to his room afterwards on another matter, he said to me: 'You are a blackguard. You ought to have put it to me'. I have never been so treated in my life. He had many good points: but when he was upset about anything, he could be very rude to counsel at the bar. Just as he was to me. So much so that some declined to appear before him.

1. Cmnd. 6945.
2. Cmnd. 7024.

6 Things have changed now

Things have changed greatly now. In my days in the Divorce Division, everything centred round the matrimonial offence. A vast complex of law was developed on adultery, cruelty, desertion, connivance, collusion. Cases went on for days and days at great expense so as to find who was to blame for the breakdown of the marriage. For so much depended on it. Both parties might want a divorce, but they would contest the case to the bitter end: for on the outcome might depend the custody of the children, access to them, maintenance of the wife, and so forth. All that has changed now. No longer do the Courts inquire which of the two is to blame. If the marriage has irretrievably broken down, a divorce can be had for the asking. No need even to go to the Court. It can be done by affidavit by post. Very few divorce petitions are contested. The divorce itself goes through undefended. The contest is afterwards in chambers. There the parties argue on property rights and on the custody of children. It is to these that the law directs its attention. But, before considering them, I would tell you more of the story by which women have become equal to men.

2 The story of emancipation

After the Report of the Divorce Committee, I was invited to become President of the National Marriage Guidance Council. It has done great work in the shape of reconciliation and of education for marriage. I gave an address to them in 1950 in which I outlined the past and looked to the future.

1 The difference

No matter how you may dispute and argue, you cannot alter the fact that women are different from men. The principal task in life of women is to bear and rear children: and it is a task which occupies the best years of their lives. The man's part in bringing up the children is no doubt as important as hers, but of necessity he cannot devote so much time to it. He is physically the stronger and she the weaker. He is temperamentally the more aggressive and she the more submissive. It is he who takes the initiative and she who responds. These diversities of function and temperament lead to differences of outlook which cannot be ignored. But they are, none of them, any reason for putting women under the subjection of men. A woman feels as keenly, thinks as clearly, as a man. She in her sphere does work as useful as man does in his. She has as much right to her freedom – to develop her personality to the full – as a man. When she marries, she does not become the husband's servant but his equal partner. If his work is more important in the life of the community, hers is more important in the life of the family.

Neither can do without the other. Neither is above the other or under the other. They are equals.

Few will dispute the justice of woman's claim to equality: but it is only in recent years that it has been realised. This is one of the most significant revolutions of our time. It has tremendous potentialities for our civilisation.

2 The past

It is only a little over 100 years that woman's claim to equality has been recognised. All previous ages have treated women as inferior to men. Little thought and less money was spent on their education. Their place was in the home for which no training was necessary. When they married, they became subject to their husbands. They were unable to own anything and unable even to agree anything apart from him. They had to do as their husbands told them. All this was regarded as the natural state of affairs. Women themselves accepted it. They were brought up to believe it. The only compensation they had – or rather which some of them had – was that in some periods and in some classes men were expected to treat women with courtesy and kindness. But that only served to emphasise the superiority of man and the inferiority of woman. It showed her as dependent on the generosity which he was magnanimous enough to bestow.

Some philosophers have in times past advocated the equality of women, but they have often been regarded as unpractical theorists. It was Plato nearly 2,400 years ago (*circa* 400 BC) who first had sufficient independence of mind to assert that there should be equality. It was a remarkable thing to do, because the Athenian woman of his day was in no way the equal of her husband; she was not the entertainer of his guests or the mistress of his house, but only his housekeeper and the mother of his children. Every woman in Athens had always to remain under the tutelage of some male. Wife and daughters were kept in strict seclusion. Though custom permitted them, when attended by female slaves, to go for a walk, they would not stop to converse with men, nor would they ever attend a meal at which men guests were present[1]. In short, it was their duty always to keep in the background. A very different ideal of woman-hood was held up by Plato to the world. She was to be the companion of the man, and to share with him in the toils of war and in the cares of government. She was to be educated in the same way as he. Even as the men of Athens used to strip to do their gymnastic exercises, so should the women. 'Let the wives of our guardians strip', he said, 'for their virtue will be their robe, and let them share in the toils of war and the defence of their country; only in the distribution of the labours, the lighter are to be assigned to the women, who are the weaker natures, but in other respects their duties are to be the same'[2].

Search as you will among other philosophers, you will not find one advocating the equality of women in so enlightened a way until you come to our own John Stuart Mill, who wrote in 1869 his famous essay on 'The Subjection of Women'. That was an acute and learned plea for equality.

3 The attitude of the Church

In old times the Christian Church had much influence on current attitudes. It always insisted on the obedience of a woman to her husband. 'Wives, submit yourselves unto your husbands' said St. Paul, 'for the husband is the head of the wife . . . so let the wives be subject to their own husbands in everything'[3]; and St. Peter said: 'Likewise ye wives, be in subjection to your own husbands'[4]. Milton puts the rule in memorable words when he makes Eve address Adam thus:

'My author and disposer, what thou bidst,
Unargued I obey. So God ordains.

1. Robinson *History of Greece*, p. 368.
2. Plato *Republic*, V. 457 (Jowett's translation).
3. *Ephesians* V, 22—24.
4. I *Peter* III, 1.

God is thy law, thou mine; to know no more
Is woman's happiest knowledge and her praise'[1].

The precept found its place in the marriage service. In the prayer book as authorised by law the bride promised to obey her husband. The canon law of the Church translated this precept into a legal obligation. Lord Stowell, our greatest ecclesiastical Judge, said that 'It is the law of religion, and the law of this country, that the husband is entrusted with authority over his wife . . . . Obedience is her duty'[2]. This rule of the Church was supported by eminent philosophers with great show of reason. Sir Thomas Brown in his *Philosophy of the Human Mind* (lecture 88) said that 'It is obviously necessary that for mutual peace the will of one should be submitted to the will of the other . . . . the power of decision therefore, which for the sake of peace must be understood as resting somewhere, should rest with the man'.

The Christian Church was always strict about divorce. It always set its face against any type of divorce which permits remarriage. The texts in the Bible are themselves capable of two interpretations. There is a verse of St. Matthew V, 32 which seems to permit divorce for adultery and there has been much scholarly difference about it. Some scholars think that the phrase 'saving for the cause of fornication' is a gloss put in by a later scribe. The Christian doctrine was, however, clear. There should be no divorce, for whatever cause, however grave, so as to permit one party to remarry during the lifetime of the other. The justification for this view was that though, in particular cases, the indissolubility of marriage may operate with great severity on individuals, nevertheless the general well-being of the family and of the community is secured by maintaining it inviolate.

4 The effect on the law

The Christian Church laid down principles which had great

1. Milton *Paradise Lost*, Book IV, 1.634.
2. *I Hagg Cons*, p. 363.

effect in forming our opinions and laws upon this subject. The precepts of the Church became embodied in the canon law and thence translated into the common law. It carried out with rigorous consistency the complete legal subjection of the wife to the husband.

Let me give you a simple illustration of the influence of the Christian precepts on the law. In St. Matthew's Gospel you will remember the precept that 'a man shall leave father and mother and shall cleave to his wife: and they twain shall be one flesh'[1]. This was translated into the principle that 'by marriage the husband and wife are one person in law': and the husband was that one. That principle has had a great influence on our law. Sir William Blackstone declared that 'upon this principle of an union of person in husband and wife depend almost all the legal rights, duties and disabilities that either of them acquires by the marriage'[2]. The scope of the principle was expressed by him thus: 'The very being or legal existence of the woman is suspended during the marriage, or at least is incorporated and consolidated into that of the husband: under whose wing, protection and cover, she performs everything'.

The law took no notice of the converse precept that the husband was to love and cherish his wife. The magnanimous protector was authorised also to be a tyrant. Every husband was by law given power and dominion over his wife. It was said in the old books that he might keep her by force within the bounds of duty and might beat her, but not in a violent or cruel manner. The gloss put upon this by the common man was that he might beat her but only with a stick not thicker than his thumb. By the time that Blackstone wrote towards the end of the 18th century this power began to be doubted among the higher ranks of society: but he adds that 'the lower rank of the people, who were always fond of the old common law, still claim and exert their antient privilege; and the courts of law will still permit a husband

1. *Matthew* XIX, 5.
2. Blackstone *Commentaries*, I. 442.

to restrain a wife of her liberty in case of any gross misbehaviour'[1]. As late as 1840 when a wife threatened to leave her husband, he was held to be entitled to keep her a prisoner in the house and to use force for the purpose. It was not until 1891 that the courts gave her the right to come and go as she pleased. It was decided in a celebrated case where the husband thought he was well within the law[2]. His wife had left him and he had obtained from the courts an order that she should return to him. When she did not obey, he waited for her one Sunday morning outside the church where she had gone for the service. He had a solicitor's clerk with him, and together they bundled her into a waiting carriage and drove her off with her feet sticking out of the door. They took her to the husband's house and kept her there against her will. But one of her relatives saw her at the window – just before the blind was hastily drawn – and brought a habeas corpus. The Court ordered her release: and from that day to this it has never been doubted that a husband has no right to deprive his wife of her liberty.

I now turn from the wife's personal position to her ownership of property. We know that in the marriage service it is the man who assures the woman that 'with all my worldly goods I thee endow'; but the law did the exact opposite. Upon marriage all the woman's goods and chattels, and all her money, automatically belonged to the man save for her own personal clothing and paraphernalia. If her parents or friends gave her wedding presents, such as a writing desk or a pair of candlesticks, they belonged to the husband. If during the marriage she went out to work, all that she earned belonged automatically to her husband. Just think what great power this gave to him, and how dependent it made her. She had to go to him, on bended knee, whenever she wanted to buy anything even with her own money or her own earnings. If she left him, even for good cause, she had no right to any maintenance even out of her own funds. The only remedy which the common law gave her was that she could pledge

1. Blackstone *Commentaries*, I. 445.
2. *R v Jackson* [1891] 1 QB 671.

199

his credit for necessaries, but even then she had to find some tradesman who would supply her — and none might be willing to do so. Most tradesmen, however keen they were to do business, also wished to be sure of being paid. They did not wish to be involved in a lawsuit as to whether the wife was entitled to pledge her husband's credit or not. If they were unwilling to accept the husband's credit, it was useless for the wife to pledge her own. She had no power to contract on her own behalf, because she was one with her husband and could agree to nothing apart from him. Moreover, she had no property or money with which to honour any contract which she might make. She was in a parlous plight.

5 Parliament alters all

By a series of Acts of Parliament, however, starting in 1870, all the disabilities of wives in regard to property have been swept away. A married woman is now entitled to her own property and earnings, just as her husband is entitled to his. Her stocks and shares remain hers. Her wedding presents are hers. Her earnings are hers. She can deal with all her property as fully as any man. She can no longer be restrained from touching the capital. She can make contracts on her own account, and can sue and be sued upon them by herself alone. No longer is she dependent on her husband. She can, and does, go out to work and earn her own living. Her equality is complete.

6 The present status

In the last 90 years we have seen more progress towards equality than in the thousand years before. The women of today are the companions of men. During the war they shared in its toils. They made munitions, they drove army cars, they decoded cypher messages, they plotted the course of aircraft. They were dropped for secret service behind the enemy lines. In peacetime they work alongside men in all tasks for which they are physically suitable. They work in the factories. They patrol the streets as police. They share in the cares of government. They serve in Parliament. A woman is now our Prime Minister. They become Ministers of the Crown and Mayors of cities. They are educated in the same way as men. The girls go to boys' schools: and the boys to girls' schools. Most of the colleges at Oxford and Cambridge have both men and women. They become doctors, lawyers, writers, directors of companies, and so forth. They become Queen's Counsel and Judges. Plato's ideal is substantially attained.

Let me conclude with this one thought. This freedom which women have achieved carries with it equal responsibilities. If they live up to their responsibilities, their equality is not only a matter of absolute justice, but is also capable of great benefits to the human race: and of all their responsibilities, the chief is to maintain a sound and healthy family life in the land. To this chief responsibility all other interests must be subordinated. It is here that I depart from Plato. He would carry the equality of women so far that there were no marriages of one man with one woman, but that men and women should associate with one another as they pleased, and leave the children to be brought up by the State. If equality were to lead to such a result, it would be the end of our civilisation which is built upon a sound family life. The only basis for a sound family life is a Christian marriage — the personal union of one man with one woman, to the exclusion of all others on either side, for better or for worse, so long as both shall live.

Part seven

The deserted wife's equity

Introduction

Having thus told the general story, I would henceforward tell how the law has been developed to keep pace with it. In particular, how the judges have evolved new principles to meet the new situation. It is one of the best examples in recent times of the judicial role in Law Reform. The first – and most controversial – was the invention of the deserted wife's equity.

I confess that it was I who did it. Well supported for twelve years by my colleagues in the Court of Appeal. But scorned by commentators and in due course by the House of Lords. It is even now held up as an example of how *not* to reform the law. Yet I venture to suggest that, without our efforts, it might have taken over forty years to obtain any protection for a deserted wife. It was only in 1978 that the Law Commission made their Report on the Matrimonial Home (Co-ownership and Occupation Rights)[1]: and we have yet to see a Bill before Parliament to implement it.

1. Cmnd. 450. See p. 246, post.

1 Invoking Section 17 of the 1882 Act

1 A case in chambers

In Cervantes' satire *Don Quixote* you can read of the Knight-errant. He wandered about the world in search of opportunities of rescuing damsels in distress. So also will some make fun of me in respect of deserted wives. Like Don Quixote 'revenging all kinds of injuries, and offering himself to occasions and dangers, which, being once happily achieved, might gain him eternal renown'[1].

It all started when I was a King's Bench Judge sitting in chambers in November 1947. 'In chambers' is our old-fashioned word for a set of rooms. According to the Shorter Oxford Dictionary it is 'the room in which a Judge sits to transact minor business'. In my time it was one judge only two days a week, Tuesdays and Fridays. Now it is two or three judges five days a week. All sorts of 'minor business' about pleadings, interim orders, and so forth. The public are not allowed in. It is not important enough.

2 A piece of minor business

On this occasion it was 'minor business' about possession of a house. It belonged to a husband. The deeds were in his name. He had bought it 15 years before and had lived in it with his wife and invalid son. But during the war he had left her and gone off to live with another woman. He had bought another house and set up in it with the other woman. The

1. Cervantes *Don Quixote* (Skelton's translation 1612).

206

wife got an order for maintenance against the husband. It was fixed at a modest sum on the basis that the wife could continue living in the matrimonial home with the invalid son. But the husband wanted the wife to divorce him. She refused. He said: 'I'll give you the house if you will give me my freedom'. She still refused to divorce him. So he took proceedings to turn her out of the house. That might make her change her mind.

The case came before a Master of the King's Bench. He is one of the lower echelon of judges dealing with so-called 'minor business', but often very important to the parties. In this case the Master could see no answer to the husband's claim. The house belonged to the husband. He had the title to it. She had no right to it. She was not a tenant or anything of that sort. So he made an order for possession.

3 The first deserted wife comes before me

It came on appeal to me. The wife was represented by a very learned counsel, Michael Stranders. He had looked up a lot of cases. The husband was represented by a good but un-learned counsel, Charles Rochford. He had looked up very few. I could see that here was an injustice. It cried aloud for a remedy. I could see that it was of the first importance. So I decided not to give judgment in chambers – where it would not be reported. But to give it in open Court, where it could be reported. I did not cite a single case. I dealt with it simply on principle. As it happened, it was missed by the regular series of Law Reports. It was only in the *Times Law Reports*. It is reported as *H v H*[1]. This is what I said:

'It is contended for the husband that, as he is the owner of the house, I must make the order for which he asks. On behalf of the wife it is argued that I have a discretion in the matter. In my opinion, at common law the husband has no right to turn the wife out of the house. It was the house which he provided as the matrimonial home. She has behaved

1. (1947) 63 TLR 645 at 646.

quite properly. She has done nothing wrong. He cannot sue her for ejectment, or trespass or for any other tort. He has no right in law to claim possession from her except such as may be given him by section 17 of the Married Women's Property Act 1882. But that section does not, in my opinion, give him the right which he is now claiming. It enacts that the Judge before whom the application comes may make such order as he thinks fit. The intention is that in the innumerable and infinitely various disputes as to property which may occur between husband and wife the Judge should have a free hand to do what is just. That discretion is in no way fettered, though it must be exercised judicially.

'. . . . Applying the discretion vested in me in that section I am satisfied that it would be unjust to turn the respondent and the son out, and I decline to make the order for which the husband asks. The appeal will be allowed, with costs'.

So I proceeded myself on the very words of section 17 of the Married Women's Property Act 1882. In case of any question between husband and wife as to the title to or possession of property, that section authorised any judge of the High Court to 'make such order with respect to the property in dispute as he thinks fit'. I stressed the words 'as he thinks fit'. I held that these words gave the judge 'a free hand to do what is just'. It was a principle which I sought to apply in many later cases. Notably in *Hine v Hine*[1] where I said:

'It seems to me that the jurisdiction of the Court over family assets is entirely discretionary. Its discretion transcends all rights, legal or equitable, and enables the Court to make such order as it thinks fit. This means, as I understand it, that the Court is entitled to make such order as may be fair and just in all the circumstances of the case'.

4 My principle is overturned

But alas, the principle did not survive the scrutiny of the House of Lords. It took over 20 years before it was finally

1. [1962] 1 WLR 1124 at 1127.

scotched in *Pettitt v Pettitt*[1]. The House there declared that section 17 was procedural only. It did not affect the legal rights of either party. In every case the court has to inquire what are the legal rights of the parties and give effect to them – without exercising any discretion in the matter. Quoting my principle and condemning it, Lord Hodson said (at page 808):

'To use the language of Coke, this would be to substitute the uncertain and crooked cord of discretion for the golden and straight metwand of the law (First Institute p. 41)'.

1. [1970] AC 777.

2 Invoking the aid of equity

1 Equity comes to the rescue

Thus my principle was overturned. Yet there was to hand another way of defeating the husband's claim to possession. It was by giving to the deserted wife a right to be in the house. If she was armed with such a right, she could say to her husband: 'Although the title stands in your name, I have a right on my own account to stay here'. Not only could she claim it as against her husband. But if he sold the house over her head, she could claim it as against the purchaser. That is the way some husbands tried to get their wives out. One husband sold the house to his new mistress and got it vested in her name. The mistress then sued the wife for possession. But the wife was able to say, and did say: 'I have a right to be here. It is given to me by equity. It is the deserted wife's equity'.

2 A junior wins his spurs

There was a great case in which we established this equity: or rather we thought we established it. Like so many of our attempts, it was afterwards rejected by the House of Lords. But it is worth remembering. It was *Bendall v McWhirter*[1]. Thus husband was the freehold owner of the house where he lived with his wife and children. He deserted her but before he went, he said to her: 'You can have the house and furniture'. She got a maintenance order against him of £4 10s a

1. [1952] 2 QB 466.

week on the basis that she could stay in the house. He afterwards went bankrupt. The trustee in bankruptcy wanted to
sell the house and divide the proceeds among the creditors.
But, to get a full price, he wanted to sell it with vacant
possession. So he asked her to vacate. She refused. He
brought an action against her for possession. The county
court Judge ordered her out. She appealed to the Court of
Appeal. She was represented by Mr. Muir Hunter, then a
junior at the bar. He won his spurs here. He had specialised
in the law of bankruptcy but he showed in this case – and in
later cases – that he was no mere specialist. He has won
distinction since in many fields. It was his mastery of details
that led to the discovery of the frauds of John Poulson and
his subsequent conviction. We allowed the appeal of the
deserted wife. We held that she had a right to stay in the
house and that the trustee in bankruptcy of her husband
could not evict her. This is what I said (at page 475):

'The first question on the facts is whether the wife has any
right of her own to stay in the house. Under the old common
law as it existed until 70 years ago she had no rights at all
apart from those of her husband. She was treated by the
law more like a piece of his furniture than anything else. The
husband could not sue her in ejectment or trespass, but
neither could he sue a piece of furniture. He could bundle
his furniture out into the street, and so he could his wife. The
law did not say him nay. It merely gave the wife authority to
pledge his credit for necessaries. If her husband turned her
out, she had to go and find lodgings elsewhere, pledging his
credit for the rent, that is, if she could find anyone to trust
to his credit. She could not in those days get an order for
maintenance against her husband. She had to find someone
who would take her in out of pity or charity or on the
husband's credit. She could not pledge her own credit for
she could not make a contract. Even if the husband did not
turn her out, nevertheless when he ceased for any reason to
be entitled to the house she would have to leave it: for she
had no right of her own to stay there. Thus, if the husband

became bankrupt his assignees in bankruptcy could turn her out just as they could his furniture.

'All that has changed now. A wife is no longer her husband's chattel. She is beginning to be regarded by the law as a partner in all affairs which are their common concern. Thus the husband can no longer turn her out of the matrimonial home. She has as much right as he to stay there even though the house does stand in his name. This has only been decided in the last ten years. It started in 1942 when Goddard LJ said that the husband's only way of getting his wife out of the house was to make an application under section 17 of the Married Women's Property Act 1882: see *Bramwell v Bramwell*[1]. That section gives the court a very wide discretion in the matter; and accordingly, in 1947, when a husband claimed that he had an absolute right to turn his wife out, it was held that he had no such right, but that it was a matter for the discretion of the court: see *H v H*[2]. Very shortly afterwards, this court took the same view (*Stewart v Stewart*[3]), and it is now settled law that a deserted wife has a right, as against her husband, to stay in the matrimonial home unless and until an order is made against her under section 17. In support of this right His Honour Judge Willes recently made an order allowing a wife to stay until the husband found alternative accommodation, and restraining the husband from selling the house over her head, and we affirmed it: *Lee v Lee*[4]. Moreover it has been held that the wife's right is effective, not only as against her husband but also as against the landlord. Thus where a husband, who was statutory tenant of the matrimonial home, deserted his wife and left the house, it was held that the landlord could not turn her out so long as she paid the rent and performed the conditions of the tenancy. . . .

'What is the nature of this right of the deserted wife which the courts have thus evolved? It bears, I think, a very close resemblance to her right to pledge her husband's credit for

1. [1942] 1 KB 370 at 374.
2. (1947) 63 TLR 645.
3. [1948] 1 KB 507 at 513.
4. [1952] 2 QB 489.

necessaries. Under the old common law, when a husband deserted his wife, or they separated owing to his misconduct, she had an irrevocable authority to pledge his credit for necessaries: *Boulton v Prentice*[1], quoted in the notes to *Manby v Scott*[2]. One of the most obvious necessaries of a wife is a roof over her head; and if we apply the old rule to modern conditions it seems only reasonable to hold that when the husband is the tenant of the matrimonial home, the wife should have an irrevocable authority to continue the tenancy on his credit; and that when he is the owner of it she should have an irrevocable authority to stay there. This authority, like the old one, is based on an irrebuttable presumption of law. . .'.

Then I turned to the real problem in this case. It was whether the right of the deserted wife was binding on his successors in title, that is, on those who bought the house from him or on his trustee in bankruptcy. This is how I finished (page 484):

'. . . . I should have thought the court would have a discretion whether to order possession or not, for that is the only way in which effect can be given to the wife's right as now established. Any other view would lead to great injustice. It would mean that a guilty husband could transfer the house into the name of his new mistress and then get her to evict his innocent lawful wife from the matrimonial home. No civilised community could tolerate such a cynical disregard of the married state. Equity demands that the successor in title should be in no better position than the husband.

'The result of the whole case is that the wife's right to stay in the matrimonial home does not come to an end automatically on the husband's bankruptcy. The trustee in bankruptcy takes subject to equities. He takes therefore subject to her right, for it is an equity. The trustee must apply to the court for possession, and the judge who hears the case

1. 1 Selw NP (13th edn), 233.
2. 2 *Smith's Leading Cases* (13th edn), 456 at 469.

will take into account the various competing interests. . . .

'In my opinion the appeal should succeed and judgment be entered for the wife'.

3 An outcry amongst the purists

This decision produced an outcry amongst the purists, especially my Chancery colleagues. The most vigorous protest came from one of the most able and learned minds of the time and the most expressive. It was my friend R. E. Megarry, then still a junior but afterwards to become Vice-Chancellor of England. He wrote an article in *The Law Quarterly Review* (of which he afterwards became editor). It is in the issue for July 1952 (68 LQR 379). In it he said:

'One of the most lusty infants to which English law has given birth in recent years is the right of a deserted wife to remain in occupation of the matrimonial home owned by her husband notwithstanding his desire to evict her. . . .

. . . .

'. . . . It may well be that justice requires that the wife's occupation of the home should be protected in some special way; and modern ideas of sex equality may require that the right should not be exclusively feminine in gender. Yet with all respect it may be suggested that legislation and not litigation is the only satisfactory way of delimiting the bounds of so complex a subject. Any protection for the wife should, it is suggested, be provided by statutory amendments of the matrimonial law operating on the recognised rights of property, rather than by what is (in effect, at all events) the judicial invention of a new proprietary right. . . . Few would suggest that the law as to this new-found right of the wife is at present in a satisfactory state, and some, indeed, may express the hope that the House of Lords will blow away the whole uncertain structure . . . at least it may be hoped that the right will ultimately be held not to amount, either in name or in substance, to any legal or equitable interest in land, and to bind none save the husband'.

3 The Lords triumphant

1 The deserted wife is taken to the Lords

That was in 1952. It took 13 years before a case did reach the House of Lords; and then the House did do what Mr. Megarry had invited them to do. He laid the cable leading to the explosive charge. They pressed the handle which set it off. It blew the deserted wife's equity to smithereens. And me with it. For I had presided in the Court of Appeal. It was in *National Provincial Bank v Hastings Car Mart Ltd*[1]. The husband owned a dwellinghouse where he lived with his wife and children. He deserted her and lived with another woman. Then he went through an ingenious scheme. He formed his business into his own private limited company, The Hastings Car Mart Ltd. He also transferred the matrimonial home to the new company. Then the new company borrowed money from the National Provincial Bank for the purposes of its business: and in support of the overdraft the new company charged the matrimonial home to the Bank. The new company did not pay off the overdraft. The Bank came down on the wife. They said that they required to enforce their charge on the property and, in order to do so, required the property to be vacated. She refused to give up possession. She relied on the 'deserted wife's equity' which appeared now to be well established. In the Court of Appeal we refused the Bank's claim. I said (at page 683):

'Since the war there have been many cases in this court which have established that a wife, who has been deserted by her

1. [1964] Ch 665.

husband, has a right to remain in occupation of the matrimonial home unless and until the court orders her to go. The
development can be easily traced. Prior to the war it was
recognised that, where the husband owns the matrimonial
home and is living there himself, he cannot turn his wife
out. He cannot treat her as a stranger. He cannot exclude
her from the house without good cause. See *Shipman v
Shipman*[1], by Atkin LJ. Now suppose he deserts his wife
and goes off, leaving her in the matrimonial home with the
children. Is he to be in any better position because he has
deserted her? Can he turn her out as if she was a stranger?
Clearly not. He cannot take advantage of his own wrong — of
his own desertion — and use it as a ground for ejecting her.
The reason is simply this: it is the husband's duty to provide
the wife with a roof over her head; and, by providing the
matrimonial home, he gives her an authority to be there. It
is an authority which he cannot revoke, so long as it remains
the matrimonial home. He certainly cannot revoke it on his
desertion. Just as in olden days a deserted wife had an
irrevocable authority to pledge his credit for necessaries, so
in these days she has an irrevocable authority to remain in
the matrimonial home. It is revocable only by order of the
court: see *Jess B. Woodcock & Sons Ltd v Hobbs*[2].

'. . . . The right is now so well established that it is not
open to question. It has received the commendation of the
Royal Commission on Marriage and Divorce (Cmnd. 9678
(1956), p. 180). They said (in para. 664): "We think it has
been right to afford this protection to a deserted wife, to
allow her to keep a roof over her head; it would be shocking
to contemplate that a husband could put his wife and children into the street, so that he could himself return to live in
the home, perhaps with another woman".

'But the question here is: What is the position of successors
in title? Suppose the husband, after deserting his wife, sells
the house over her head, or mortgages it without her knowledge. Can the purchaser or mortgagee turn her out? The

1. [1924] 2 Ch 140 at 146, 40 TLR 483, CA.
2. [1955] 1 All ER 445, [1955] 1 WLR 152, CA.

courts have already given some consideration to the problem. Take first the case where the husband becomes bankrupt and the property becomes vested in his trustee in bankruptcy. Can the trustee turn her out and sell the house for the benefit of the creditors? This court has held that the trustee stands in no better position than the husband and cannot turn her out: see *Bendall v McWhirter*[1]. Take then the case where the husband sells the house to his new mistress for an agreed price. Can the mistress turn her out? It would be surprising if she could. Lynskey J held that the new mistress cannot turn out the wife: see *Street v Denham*[2]; *Churcher v Street*[3]. Take next the case where the husband conveys the house to a purchaser, by a genuine conveyance and no sham, but intending that the purchaser should sue the wife for possession. In one case he conveyed it to his brother-in-law; in another to a speculator. Can such a purchaser turn out the wife? The judges have held that he cannot do so: see *Ferris v Weaven*[4], *Savage v Hubble*[5]. Take finally this case, where the husband conveys the house to a company, which is entirely under his control, in return for fully paid shares. Can the company turn out the wife? Cross J thought it inconceivable. "I cannot think, however", he said,[6] "that any court would allow the company to turn Mrs. Ainsworth out of the house without providing her with another home".

'Such being the decided cases, what is the principle underlying them? It is the way of English law to decide particular cases and then seek for the principle. . . . In all these cases, if the wife has no right to remain there, the husband is fully entitled to sell the house to a purchaser or to give it away, even though the design of both is that the purchaser or donee should evict her for their own benefit. It is only because she has a right to remain that it is unlawful to enter into an arrangement designed to turn her out. Take

1. [1952] 2 QB 466, [1952] 1 All ER 1307, [1952] 1 TLR 1332.
2. [1954] 1 All ER 532, [1954] 1 WLR 624.
3. [1959] Ch 251, [1959] 1 All ER 23, [1959] 2 WLR 66.
4. [1952] WN 318, [1952] 2 All ER 233.
5. [1953] CPL 416.
6. [1963] 2 WLR 1015 at 1021.

this simple instance: Suppose the husband says to a prospective purchaser: "I cannot myself turn out my wife because I have deserted her; but if you buy from me, there is nothing to stop you getting her out, and then you can sell with vacant possession". If such a transaction were permitted, the husband would benefit greatly because he would get a high price at his wife's expense. There is nothing wrong with such a transaction if the wife has no right to remain. But there is everything wrong with it if she has a right. It seems to me that, if the cases I have mentioned were correctly decided, as I believe them to be, it can only be on the footing that the wife *has a right* to remain in the matrimonial home — and a right which is enforceable against the successors of the husband — save, of course, a purchaser for value without notice.

. . . .

'The question remains: What order should be made? When should the wife go? It is a matter for the discretion of the court. On the one hand there is the bank who desire to recoup themselves all that is owing to them. On the other hand there is the wife with four children, receiving nothing from her husband, and on National Assistance. Of all the creditors of the husband, she has the most crying claim of all. It is a case where I would fain temper justice with mercy. Justice to the bank, with mercy to the wife. . .'.

2 The Lords blow up the deserted wife

The Bank appealed to the House of Lords. They were unanimous in holding that a deserted wife had no equity to remain in the matrimonial home — as against anyone to whom the husband sold it or charged it. It is reported in *National Provincial Bank v Ainsworth*[1]. Even though the purchaser who bought it, or the bank who took a charge on it, had full knowledge that the wife was living in the house with the children — deserted by her husband — nevertheless she could be turned out. They overruled all our

1. [1965] AC 1175.

cases of long standing and in particular *Bendall v McWhirter*[1] which had stood since 1952. All they allowed to remain was this simple proposition: If the husband remained himself as the sole owner of the house — with the title in him — he could not himself turn her out. She had a personal right — as against her husband — but she had no equity — no right at all — against anyone else.

1. [1952] 2 QB 466.

4 Lady Summerskill takes charge

1 Uproar follows

In many circles there was uproar at the decision of the Lords. There was pressure on all hands for legislation to reverse it. Baroness Summerskill took a leading part. She was one of the first ladies to be made a baroness in her own right. It was in 1961. She was prominent in the feminist cause. She was active in debate. On 4 May 1966 she introduced a Bill to 'amend the law of England and Wales as to the right of a husband or wife to occupy a dwelling-house which has been the matrimonial home'.

The Bill was very valuable. It made it clear that a deserted wife had a right to stay in the matrimonial home. But it only gave her this right subject to a very important limitation. She was only protected as against a purchaser if she had registered a charge in the Land Register. I protested at this particular clause. I spoke in the debate against it on this simple ground: When a wife is deserted, she does not go at once and register a charge. She has no solicitor to advise her. She knows nothing of the Land Register. She stays weeping at home waiting for her husband to return.

This is what I said in the House in the Second Reading[1]:

'. . . . As this House has declared judicially, the law is that even though the purchaser knows exactly that the wife has been deserted, knows all about the situation when he purchases, yet the wife can be turned out. I am glad — and

1. 275 HL Official Report (5th Series) 14 June 1966, col. 44.

I hope that this House will be also — that this Bill removes this injustice.

. . . .

'Clause 2 is, I think, the one which deals with the problem I mentioned, the question of the purchaser, the person who buys from the husband and seeks to turn the wife out. As I have said, the law is that even though he knows the wife is there and has been deserted, he can turn her out. What this provision says is that the wife will be protected if before this purchase she goes and registers her charge as a charge on the Land Register. My Lords, just think. This is why I have hesitated. Is the poor wife who has not resorted to lawyers and who remains in the house hoping that her deserting husband will return, always at hand, always likely to go to a solicitor and say, "Please register this as a charge on the Land Register"? Unless she does so, she has no protection. I welcome the fact that immediately after the marriage the wife can go along and register the charge. I would recommend strongly that in future all wives, whenever their matrimonial home is bought in the husband's name, immediately, without waiting for any trouble to arise, should go and register their right in case in the future something should go wrong with the marriage. Otherwise, as the Bill stands, it is only if the wife gets in her charge in time before the husband sells that she is to be protected. . .'.

2 The Class F charge

My plea was unavailing. The Bill became law with the clause still in it. It took about a year to do it. It was enacted on 27 July 1967 as the Matrimonial Homes Act 1967. Nevertheless, despite my fears, the Act has proved of the greatest value to deserted wives. Most of them go in good time to a solicitor and register under the Land Charges Act a 'Class F' charge which is 'a charge affecting any land by virtue of the Matrimonial Homes Act 1967'.

So ends the story of the deserted wife. Her equity — a

221

judicial innovation — was destroyed: but, by legislation, a Class F charge was created to replace it. It is a good result.

3 Not a 'bare wife'

All that controversy about a 'deserted wife' arose out of the fact that the husband was the legal owner of the house. It was in his name alone. She had no legal right or interest in it. She was a 'bare wife'. Hence the attempt to clothe her with an 'equity'. It was altogether different when she was joint owner with her husband. That is becoming very common nowadays. When a young couple buy a house, the solicitors always advise them to have it in joint names. No difficulty arises then if the husband deserts her. He cannot turn her out: because she has a legal right to remain. He cannot sell the house over her head: because the sale has to be by both of them together. No protection being needed, there was no provision in the Matrimonial Homes Act 1967 about her.

But it was discovered that she did need protection. A wife and her husband bought a house in joint names and lived there with their four children. Then she left the house, taking her children with her. She did it because her husband had treated her and the children with extreme cruelty. Her husband stayed in the house with a friend. She moved into two rooms. But the conditions there were so cramped and squalid that the welfare officer advised that there was only one solution: and that was to get the husband and his friend out of the house: and for the wife to move back in with the children. She took proceedings to get him out. It was in the Southampton County Court before Judge Michael Lee — a judge wise and considerate. He ordered the husband out of the house, even though he had a legal title as joint owner. The case is *Gurasz v Gurasz*[1]. We affirmed it and I said:

'Some features of family life are elemental in our society. One is that it is the husband's duty to provide his wife with a roof over her head: and the children too. So long as the

1. [1970] P 11.

wife behaves herself, she is entitled to remain in the matrimonial home. The husband is not at liberty to turn her out of it, neither by virtue of his command, nor by force of his conduct. If he should seek to get rid of her, the court will restrain him. If he should succeed in making her go, the court will restore her. In an extreme case, if his conduct is so outrageous as to make it impossible for them to live together, the court will order him to go out and leave her there.

. . . .

'What then is the position in this case? In the first place, the wife has a proprietary right in the house. She is joint owner with her husband. By virtue of her joint ownership, she has a right to occupy the house by herself and her children. The courts can certainly enforce that right by allowing her to re-enter the house and by preventing the husband from interfering with her exercise of that right. It is true, of course, that the husband is also a joint owner, and by virtue thereof, the husband has a right to occupy it. But that is a right which the courts, for the protection of the wife, can restrict: just as it can restrict his right if he were sole owner. Such a power to restrict arises out of her personal right, as a wife, to occupy the house. If his conduct is so outrageous as to make it impossible for them to live together, the court can restrain him from using the house even though he is a joint owner.

. . . .

'Seeing that she has these rights, I think that the county court judge in this case was entitled to order the husband to vacate the house, and to allow the wife and children to return'.

4 'Battered wives'

That last was a case of a 'battered wife'. It shows how the common law itself was able to protect her. But it was the Legislature which put the finishing touches to this development. By a short Act entitled the Domestic Violence Act

1976 it enabled the County Courts to grant injunctions to protect a 'battered wife' even though the house was in the husband's sole name and it belonged to him without her having a share in it. She could get an order excluding him from the house: and even have him arrested if it was necessary for her protection. During the passage of the Bill, there was inserted a provision giving like protection to a man's mistress — in cases where they were living with each other in the same house as husband and wife. In short, protection for the woman who is commonly but erroneously called a 'common law wife'. The common law never recognised such a person. I would like to see the phrase abandoned: but it is too late now. It is commonplace. There was much controversy as to whether the Act gave her as much protection as it did to a real wife. But in the Court of Appeal in *Davis v Johnson*[1] we held, by a majority, that she was likewise protected: and the House of Lords upheld the decision.

1. [1979] AC 264.

Part eight

The wife's share in the home

1 The judges introduce it

1 A silent revolution

Whilst all the talk was taking place about 'deserted wives', there was a silent revolution going on. It was destined to be of great help to all wives: and not only to those who were deserted. It was to give her a share in the matrimonial home even though it stood in his name alone. It reminds me of the metaphor of Arthur Hugh Clough:

'For while the tired waves, vainly breaking,
    Seem here no painful inch to gain,
Far back, through creeks and inlets making,
    Comes silent, flooding in, the main'.

It is all the result of the modern ways of young married couples. Husband and wife both go out to work and earn money. They buy a house with the aid of a mortgage from a building society. It is taken in the husband's name alone. The husband pays the wife money for housekeeping. They pool their resources for their joint needs. Some goes to pay the instalments to the building society. Some for the children's clothes. Some on the car. Some on holidays. Then the marriage breaks up. One or other leaves. The house has gone up greatly in value. It may have to be sold: or one or other may still live in it with the children. To whom does it belong?

2 The sailor gets a share in the proceeds

It came up for direct decision in *Rimmer v Rimmer*[1]. The husband was a sailor in the merchant service. The wife went

1. [1953] 1 QB 63.

out to work. He allotted to her £4 a week. She earned £3 10s a week. She used £280 of her money to pay the instalments to the building society, and she used his money to pay the housekeeping expenses. Later he deserted her. He said it was his house as it was in his name. He turned her out and sold it with vacant possession for over £2,000. She claimed that, in equity, the proceeds of sale should be paid to her. She had paid the purchase price of the house by paying the instalments to the building society. The husband claimed the proceeds of sale because the house belonged to him. Before the war undoubtedly the husband would have been entitled to it all: because it was his property. The wife could have claimed nothing because she had no contract giving her any part of it. (Such was the ground of the decision in *Hoddinott v Hoddinott*[1] where I dissented.) But in this case of *Rimmer v Rimmer* we struck out on a new line. We were quite conscious of it. We held that the proceeds should be divided equally. I put it in this way[2]:

'In 1882, when Parliament declared that a wife was entitled to have property of her own, it enacted that in any question between husband and wife as to the title to or possession of property, the court was to decide the matter as it thought fit. Parliament laid down no principles for the guidance of the courts, but left them to work out the principles themselves. That is being done. In cases when it is clear that the beneficial interest in the matrimonial home, or in the furniture, belongs to one or other absolutely, or it is clear that they intended to hold it in definite shares, the court will give effect to their intention: see *In re Rogers' Question*[3]; but when it is not clear to whom the beneficial interest belongs, or in what proportions, then, in this matter, as in others, equality is equity. In *Newgrosh v Newgrosh*[4] some furniture was bought by the husband's father with his own money for the use of the couple, but the receipt was taken in the wife's

1. [1949] 2 KB 406.
2. [1953] 1 QB 63 at 73.
3. [1948] 1 All ER 328.
4. (1950), 100 L Jo 525.

name. Willmer J held that the furniture belonged to them jointly, and his decision was affirmed by this court. In *Jones v Maynard*[1] a banking account was in the husband's name but was fed by the moneys of both and treated as a joint account. Vaisey J held that, although the husband's contributions were much larger than the wife's, it belonged to them both jointly.

'In this case I look on the money which was paid by the wife to the building society as money saved by their joint efforts and applied for their common benefit. I do not regard the sum of £280 as wholly the wife's money. She, no doubt, regarded it as her money because it came out of her own earnings, but it must be remembered that she was keeping herself all the time on her husband's money. The wife here, like many wives, managed the family income. She in fact used the husband's money to pay the housekeeping expenses and saved her own money. But she might equally well, and with more justice, have paid some of the housekeeping expenses out of her own money and saved a corresponding amount of the husband's money. If she had done that, some of the husband's money would presumably have gone to make up the £280 to repay the building society. Whilst they were living together, of course, it did not matter. The important thing was to pay off the mortgage and it did not matter out of whose money it was paid. When they separate, years afterwards, the husband must be given some credit for the £280, seeing that it was only by using his money for housekeeping that she was enabled to save so much of her own. It was really saved by their joint efforts, and not by hers alone; and it was applied for their common benefit. The proceeds of it should therefore belong to them both jointly. It is rather like the case when the husband only goes out to work and the wife looks after the house. If she manages to save money out of the housekeeping allowance sufficient to buy furniture for the home, which is intended to be a continuing provision for them both, then that furniture does not belong to her absolutely, even though it is

1. [1951] Ch 572.

bought in her name; nor does it belong absolutely to the husband, even though he provides the housekeeping allowance. It is the result of their joint efforts and is presumed to belong to them jointly. . . .

'. . . . It seems to me that when the parties, by their joint efforts, save money to buy a house, which is intended as a continuing provision for them both, then the proper presumption is that the beneficial interest belongs to them both jointly. The property may be bought in the name of the husband alone, or in the name of the wife alone, but nevertheless if it is bought with money saved by their joint efforts, and it is impossible fairly to distinguish between the efforts of the one and the other, then the beneficial interest should be presumed to belong to them both jointly. That is this case. I agree with my Lord that the proper presumption in regard to this house was that it was held jointly and the beneficial interest should be divided equally between them'.

3 The airman's wife gets a share in the house itself

That was only the beginning: but the principle was capable of great expansion. The house there had been sold and turned into money. The next step was when it had not been sold but remained in hand unsold. That was what happened when an airman had a house in his own name, but his wife had made substantial contributions. They fell out but both stayed on in the house, occupying separate rooms. To whom did it then belong? For the husband, it was asserted that the house went with the title to the husband. Such was the argument put by Mr. Tolstoy in *Fribance v Fribance*[1]. He was very knowledgeable and had written a book about it. He said (at page 386) that

'the wife had no right to the house or any share in it unless she could show a contract by the husband with her or a gift by him to her or a trust by him for her in regard to it'.

1. [1957] 1 WLR 384.

I said (at page 387):

'I do not think that line of argument is valid today. . . .
'. . . . In many cases, however, the intention of the parties is
not clear, for the simple reason that they never formed an
intention: so the court has to attribute an intention to them.
This is particularly the case with the family assets, by which
I mean the things intended to be a continuing provision for
them during their joint lives, such as the matrimonial home
and the furniture in it. When these are acquired by their joint
efforts during the marriage, the parties do not give a thought
to future separation. They do not contemplate divorce. They
contemplate living in the house and using the furniture
together for the rest of their lives. They buy the house and
furniture out of their available resources without worrying
too much as to whom it belongs. The reason is plain. So long
as they are living together, it does not matter which of them
does the saving and which does the paying, or which of them
goes out to work or which looks after the home, so long as
the things they buy are used for their joint benefit. In the
present case it so happened that the wife went out to work
and used her earnings to help run the household and buy the
children's clothes, whilst the husband saved. It might very
well have been the other way round. The husband might
have allotted to the wife enough money to cover all the
housekeeping and the children's clothes, and the wife might
have saved her earnings. The title to the family assets does
not depend on the mere chance of which way round it was. It
does not depend on how they happened to allocate their
earnings and their expenditure. The whole of their resources
were expended for their joint benefit – either in food and
clothes and living expenses for which there was nothing to
see or in the house and furniture which are family assets –
and the product should belong to them jointly. It belongs
to them in equal shares. I agree with Mr. Tolstoy that the
title to the property must remain the same, whether the
question arises under section 17 before divorce, or in other
proceedings after divorce, or under a will: but I think that in

each case the principles laid down in *Rimmer v Rimmer*[1] apply'.

It was in that case that I first used the term 'family assets' to cover such things as the matrimonial home and the furniture — which are provided by one or other or both as a continuing provision for the family. But it came in for rough treatment by the House of Lords. In *Pettitt v Pettitt*[2] Lord Upjohn said that the expression 'family assets' is devoid of legal meaning and its use can define no legal rights or obligations. But it has proved so useful that the Law Commission have themselves used it: and that is commendation enough.

4 Making improvements in the house

In all the cases up to this stage the wife had made contributions in money — out of the moneys she earned at work — or from her parents — towards the furnishing of the home. There remained the important question when she made contributions in money's worth by making improvements in the house itself. Often enough it happens that, when a house is in the wife's name, the husband increases its value greatly by making improvements to it: or vice versa the wife does work in a house which is in the husband's name. Does such work in the house give rise to a claim on the house? In a number of cases I sought to say that under section 17 of the Married Women's Property Act 1882 the Court had a complete discretion to do what was fair: and that it might be fair to give the husband or wife (as the case may be) a share when the improvements were substantial as in *Jansen v Jansen*[3] and not merely 'do-it-yourself' jobs as in *Button v Button*[4]: and this approach was afterwards upheld by Parliament in section 37 of the Matrimonial Proceedings and Property Act 1970.

1. [1953] 1 QB 63.
2. [1970] AC 777 at 817.
3. [1965] P 478.
4. [1968] 1 WLR 457.

2 The wide principle of fairness

1 I put it too widely

But in one case I expressed myself too widely. It is a fault of mine. It was in *Appleton v Appleton*[1]. A husband appeared in person. The wife was represented by counsel. Now I find myself often in favour of ordinary folk who conduct their own cases in person. So long as they are simple and straight-forward people. Now this husband was a worker in wood — a craftsman. He carved coats of arms. The house belonged to his wife. He did a lot of work in renovating it. His wife left him, turned him out of the house and put it up for sale. He claimed a part of the proceeds. The registrar refused him any. We allowed the appeal. I said (at page 28):

'. . . . I prefer to take the simple test: What is reasonable and fair in the circumstances as they have developed, seeing that they are circumstances which no one contemplated before?'

That is the test which I had derived from section 17 of the 1882 Act and had applied in the cases about the deserted wife[2].

2 The Lords denounce the wide principle

That broad principle was applied by my colleagues in a similar case where likewise the husband was not represented. It was *Pettitt v Pettitt*[3]. The wife got legal aid and took it to the Lords[4]. Then for the first time they had an opportunity

1. [1965] 1 WLR 25.
2. See Part seven, Chapter 1 (3).
3. [1968] 1 WLR 443.
4. [1970] AC 777.

to consider all the cases decided by the Court of Appeal over the previous 20 years. They considered the principle which I sought to establish: namely, that under section 17 of the 1882 Act, the Court could do what was fair and just in all the circumstances that had happened. They held that section 17 was procedural only. It did not create any legal rights. They said that the improvements done by the husbands in *Appleton v Appleton* and *Pettitt v Pettitt* were done gratuitously without any intention of affecting the legal title to the houses. So the husbands got nothing. The wives took the improved value of the houses without paying anything for it.

3 The trust concept

1 The Lords introduce the concept of a trust

Pettitt v Pettitt[1] was followed the next year by another case
which reached the Lords – *Gissing v Gissing*[2]. In the Court
of Appeal we had applied the wide principle. We had done
what we thought was fair and just. The House of Lords
reversed us. But in the course of the judgment the Lords
opened up a way in which a wife could be given a share in
the house without any reliance on section 17 of the 1882
Act. They did it by reference to the law of trusts. That has
always been one of the most fruitful trees in the orchard
of English law. Lord Diplock opened up the way by saying
(at page 904):

'Any claim to a beneficial interest in land by a person,
whether spouse or stranger, in whom the legal estate in the
land is not vested must be based upon the proposition that
the person in whom the legal estate is vested holds it as
trustee upon trust to give effect to the beneficial interest
of the claimant as cestui que trust. The legal principles
applicable to the claim are those of the English law of trusts
and in particular, in the kind of dispute between spouses
that comes before the courts, the law relating to the creation
and operation of "resulting, implied or constructive trusts"
. . . .

   'A resulting, implied or constructive trust – and it is
unnecessary for present purposes to distinguish between
these three classes of trust – is created by a transaction

1. [1970] AC 777.
2. [1971] AC 886.

235

between the trustee and the cestui que trust in connection with the acquisition by the trustee of a legal estate in land, whenever the trustee has so conducted himself that it would be inequitable to allow him to deny to the cestui que trust a beneficial interest in the land acquired. And he will be held so to have conducted himself if by his words or conduct he has induced the cestui que trust to act to his own detriment in the reasonable belief that by so acting he was acquiring a beneficial interest in the land'.

2 The trust concept wins the day

The House gave their decision in *Gissing v Gissing*[1] on 7 July 1970. Just over a fortnight later, we adopted the trust concept and applied it in *Falconer v Falconer*[2]. The husband had made financial contribution. We held that he had a half-share in the house. I adopted the new approach in these words which have never since been questioned (page 1336):

'. . . . This sort of point was discussed in *Gissing v Gissing* [1971] AC 886, and I will try to distil what was said. The House did not overturn any of the previous cases in this court on the subject. They can, I think, still provide good guidance. But the House did make clear the legal basis for them. It stated the principles on which a matrimonial home, which stands in the name of husband or wife alone, is nevertheless held to belong to them both jointly (in equal or unequal shares). It is done, not so much by virtue of an agreement, express or implied, but rather by virtue of a trust which is *imposed* by law. The law imputes to husband and wife an intention to create a trust, the one for the other. It does so by way of an *inference* from their conduct and the surrounding circumstances, even though the parties themselves made no agreement upon it. This inference of a trust, the one for the other, is readily drawn when each has made

1. [1971] AC 886.
2. [1970] 1 WLR 1333.

a financial contribution to the purchase price or to the
mortgage instalments. The financial contribution may be
direct, as where it is actually stated to be a contribution
towards the price or the instalments. It may be *indirect*, as
where both go out to work, and one pays the housekeeping
and the other the mortgage instalments. It does not matter
which way round it is. It does not matter who pays what. So
long as there is a substantial financial contribution towards
the family expenses, it raises the inference of a trust. But
where it is insubstantial, no such inference can be drawn: see
the cases collected in the dissenting judgment of Edmund
Davies LJ in the Court of Appeal [1969] 2 Ch 85, 97, which
was upheld by the House. The House did, however, sound a
note of warning about proportions. It is not in every case
that the parties hold in equal shares. Regard must be had to
their respective contributions. This confirms the practice of
this court. In quite a few cases we have not given half-and-
half but something different'.

3 If the husband sells the house

So it was established by judicial decision that the wife who
contributes, directly or indirectly, to the purchase money
gets a share in the house. But in many cases the house still
stood in the husband's name. He was the sole legal owner.
The wife's share was only an equitable interest. It was not
registered in the Land Register. Suppose then that the
husband sold the house over her head? Or charged it to a
bank for his own debts, without telling her anything about
it? Would the purchaser or the bank take it free of the wife's
share? If so, any husband would be able easily to defeat his
wife's share.

   The point arose in two cases recently. They are reported
under *Williams & Glyn's Bank v Boland*[1]. In each case the
husband had a business and wanted to raise money for it. He
went to the bank and offered the deeds of the house as

1. [1979] 2 WLR 550.

security for it. He did not tell his wife anything about it. She had made substantial contributions to the purchase of the house and was entitled to a share in it. But the deeds were in the husband's name. The bank lent the husband the money and took a charge on the house as security for it. The bank knew that the wife was in occupation but they said nothing to her about it. Later on the business failed. The bank sought to enforce their charge. They brought proceedings to get possession of the house — to turn both husband and wife out — so as to sell it with vacant possession. The husband of course had no answer. But the wife said that she was entitled to a share in the house; that she was in actual occupation of it; and that the bank could not turn her out.

4 Will it lead to chaos?

I will not set out here the statutory provisions except to say that the argument eventually depended on whether the wife (who was living in the house with her husband) was in 'actual occupation' of the house. The judge below, Templeman J, said she was not. He said:

'In my judgment, when a mortgagor is in actual occupation of the matrimonial home, it cannot be said that his wife also is in occupation . . . .
'. . . . Any other view would lead to chaos'.

To this I made reply (page 560):

'I profoundly disagree. Such statements would have been true a hundred years ago when the law regarded husband and wife as one: and the husband as that one. But they are not true today.

'I do not think those statements can stand with the decision of this court in *Hodgson v Marks*[1]: nor with the standing of women in our society today. Most wives now are joint owners of the matrimonial home — in law or in equity — with their husbands. They go out to work just as their husbands do. Their earnings go to build up the home just as much as

1. [1971] Ch 892.

their husbands' earnings. Visit the home and you will find that she is in personal occupation of it just as much as he is. She eats there and sleeps there just as he does. She is in control of all that goes on there — just as much as he. In no respect whatever does the nature of her occupation differ from his. If he is a sailor away for months at a time, she is in actual occupation. If he deserts her, she is in actual occupation. These instances all show that "actual occupation" is matter of fact, not matter of law. It need not be single. Two partners in a business can be in actual occupation. It does not depend on title. A squatter is often in actual occupation. Taking it simply as matter of fact, I would conclude that in the cases before us the wife is in actual occupation just as the old lady Mrs. Hodgson was in *Hodgson v Marks*.

'Once it is found that a wife is in actual occupation, then it is clear that in the case of registered land, a purchaser or lender would be well advised to make inquiry of the wife. If she then discloses her rights, he takes subject to them. If she does not disclose them, he takes free of them. I see no reason why this should cause any difficulty to conveyancers. Nor should it impair the proper conduct of businesses. Anyone who lends money on the security of a matrimonial home nowadays ought to realise that the wife may have a share in it. He ought to make sure that the wife agrees to it, or to go to the house and make inquiries of her. It seems to me utterly wrong that a lender should turn a blind eye to the wife's interest or the possibility of it — and afterwards seek to turn her and the family out — on the plea that he did not know she was in actual occupation. If a bank is to do its duty, in the society in which we live, it should recognise the integrity of the matrimonial home. It should not destroy it by disregarding the wife's interest in it — simply to ensure that it is paid the husband's debt in full — with the high interest rate now prevailing. We should not give monied right priority over social justice. We should protect the position of a wife who has a share — just as years ago we protected the deserted wife. In the hope that the House of Lords will not reverse us now as it did then'.

The case is going to the Lords. We await the result with apprehension, but it will not stop the incoming tide of emancipation.

5 The outcome

So after all the silent revolution has been accomplished. The wife who makes a financial contribution is entitled to a share in the house, even though it stands in the name of her husband.

4 Where there is no financial contribution

1 The gap left by the Lords

But there remained one gap. What about the wife who does not make a financial contribution; but does her part – a very important part – by staying in the house, keeping it clean, bringing up the children, and doing the hundred and one things that wives have to do? Is she to be excluded from any share? Whilst the wife who goes out to work gets a half-share in the house? If my broad principle had been accepted – by which the Court could do what was fair and just – the Judges might have developed the law so as to give the good wife a share too. But the Lords had slammed the door in my face. They had condemned any such principle. They had stopped development on those lines.

2 The gap is filled by Parliament

There were, however, powerful forces for reform coming up. The Church of England issued a challenging paper, 'Putting Asunder'. The Law Commission under its first Chairman – the wise, gifted and eloquent Lord Scarman – issued its papers on the reform of the Divorce Laws and Matrimonial Property. Parliament enacted statutes which revolutionised the whole of our Family Law. Apropos of the wife's share in the home, there was a comprehensive provision. It enabled the Court, on or after a divorce, to make an order transferring assets from husband to wife or vice versa.

3 The judges do what is necessary

Taking advantage of this provision the judges had to explain
how it was to work. The case was *Wachtel v Wachtel*[1]. It is
one of the most important we have ever had. It was argued
before Lords Justices Phillimore, Roskill and me. The argument took three days: but we took over two months to
prepare the judgment. That is unusually long for us. We
rarely take more than two or three weeks. We each played
our part. We discussed it point by point. Each of us wrote
a portion of the judgment. Lord Justice Phillimore with his
great experience in family matters. Lord Justice Roskill
with his keen intellect and quick perception. And me just
to co-ordinate our thoughts and deliver the judgment. It sets
out the effect of the Statute (the Matrimonial Proceedings
and Property Act 1970) in words which I simply repeat, as
they cover all the ground (page 92):

'Before the Act of 1970 there might have been much debate
as to whether the wife had made financial contributions of
sufficient substance to entitle her to a share in the house. The
judge said ante, p. 8OG, that it "might have been an important
issue". We agree. But he went on to say that since the Act of
1970 it was "of little importance" because the powers of
transfer under section 4 enabled the court to do what was
just having regard to all the circumstances. We agree. We feel
sure that registrars and judges have been acting on this view:
because, whereas previously we had several cases in our list
each term under section 17 of the Married Women's Property
Act 1882: now we have hardly any.

'How is the court to exercise its discretion under the Act
of 1970 in regard to the matrimonial home? We will lead
up to the answer by tracing the way in which the law has
developed. Twenty-five years ago, if the matrimonial home
stood in the husband's name, it was taken to belong to
him entirely, both in law and in equity. The wife did not
get a proprietary interest in it simply because she helped
him to buy it or to pay the mortgage instalments. Any

1. [1973] Fam 72.

money that she gave him for these purposes would be regarded as gifts, or, at any rate, not recoverable by her: see *Balfour v Balfour*[1]. But by a long line of cases, starting with *Re Rogers' Question*[2] and ending with *Hazell v Hazell*[3], it has been held by this court that, if a wife contributes directly or indirectly, in money or money's worth, to the initial deposit or to the mortgage instalments, she gets an interest proportionate to her contribution. In some cases it is a half-share. In others less.

'The court never succeeded, however, in getting a wife a share in the house by reason of her other contributions: other, that is, than her financial contributions. The injustice to her has often been pointed out. Seven members of the *Royal Commission on Marriage and Divorce* (Cmnd. 9678) in 1956 presided over by Lord Morton of Henryton, said at p. 178:
"If, on marriage, she gives up her paid work in order to devote herself to caring for her husband and children, it is an unwarrantable hardship when in consequence she finds herself in the end with nothing she can call her own".
'In 1965, Sir Jocelyn Simon, when he was President, used a telling metaphor (see [1970] AC 777, 811): "The cock can feather the nest because he does not have to spend most of his time sitting on it". He went on to give reasons in an address which he gave to The Law Society (1965) 62 *Law Society Gazette*, 345:
"In the generality of marriages the wife bears and rears children and minds the home. She thereby frees her husband for his economic activities. Since it is her performance of her function which enables the husband to perform his, she is in justice entitled to share in its fruits".
'But the courts have never been able to do justice to her. In April 1969 in *Pettitt v Pettitt*[4], Lord Hodson said: "I do not myself see how one can correct the imbalance which may

1. [1919] 2 KB 571.
2. [1948] 1 All ER 328.
3. [1972] 1 WLR 301.
4. [1970] AC 777 at 811.

be found to exist in property rights as between husband and wife without legislation".

'Now we have legislation. In order to remedy injustice Parliament has intervened. The Act of 1970 expressly says that, in considering whether to make a transfer of property, the court is to have regard, among other things, to:
"(f) the contributions made by each of the parties to the welfare of the family, including any contributions made by looking after the home or caring for the family".

'. . . . In their *Report on Financial Provision in Matrimonial Proceedings* (Law Com. No. 25) H. of C. (1968—69) No. 448, p. 34, para. 69 the Law Commission emphasised the importance of section 5 (1) (f) and the change which it would make. They said:
"we recommend that in the exercise of the court's armoury of powers to order financial provision it should be directed to have regard to various criteria. Among these there is one of outstanding importance in regard to the adjustment of property rights as between the spouses. This is the extent to which each has contributed to the welfare of the family, including not only contributions in money or money's worth (as in the determination of rights to particular items of property) but also the contribution made (normally by the wife) in looking after the home and family. This should meet the strongest complaint made by married women, and recognised as legitimate by the Morton Commission in 1956, namely that the contribution which wives make towards the acquisition of the family assets by performing their domestic chores, thereby releasing their husbands for gainful employment, is at present wholly ignored in determining their rights. Under our proposal this contribution would be a factor which the court would be specifically directed to take into account".

'It has sometimes been suggested that we should not have regard to the reports of the Law Commission which lead to legislation. But we think we should. They are most helpful in showing the mischief which Parliament intended to remedy.

'In the light thus thrown on the reason for subsection

(1) (f), we may take it that Parliament recognised that the wife who looks after the home and family contributes as much to the family assets as the wife who goes out to work. The one contributes in kind. The other in money or money's worth. If the court comes to the conclusion that the home has been acquired and maintained by the joint efforts of both, then, when the marriage breaks down, it should be regarded as the joint property of both of them, no matter in whose name it stands. Just as the wife who makes substantial money contributions usually gets a share, so should the wife who looks after the home and cares for the family for 20 years or more'.

4 More and more equality

Apart from these property matters, there is growing apace the move for equality. We have the Equal Pay Act 1970 and the Sex Discrimination Act 1975. These were the direct result of our joining the Common Market. They were passed so as to fulfil our obligations under the Treaty of Rome. Whenever a woman does work of equal value to a man, she is entitled to pay equal to his. Whenever there is a job which she can do – she is entitled to apply for it and to get it on equal terms with a man. There must be no discrimination against her because she is a woman. Likewise there must be no discrimination against a man because he is a man. This was invoked when a bachelor Mr. Jeremiah claimed that he was put on to dirty work when the women were not. I said in *Jeremiah v Ministry of Defence*[1]:

'Equality is the order of the day. In both directions. For both sexes. What is sauce for the goose is sauce for the gander'.

1. 19 October 1979 (not yet reported).

Conclusion

Thus far has the law developed up to date. Now there are further developments looming ahead. The Law Commission have made their third Report on Family Property. It came out in June 1978 and is Command Paper No. 450. It has 408 pages. It is divided into three books. Book one recommends there should be co-ownership of the matrimonial home. Book two covers rights in respect of occupation of the matrimonial home. Book three covers use and enjoyment of the household goods.

These recommendations will no doubt form the basis of a Bill which will be laid before Parliament. They appear to be in accord with the wide principles which we have tried to introduce by judicial decision. They eliminate the restrictions made by the House of Lords. They have the merit that they go into many details that have not hitherto come before the courts for decision. If passed into law, it will mean that the role of the judges will in future be confined to the interpretation of the Statute. But it is judges hitherto who have been the pioneers.

Epilogue

This last has been an exciting year. On my 80th birthday, 23 January 1979, on my way down Chancery Lane for the newspaper (regularly at 7.45 a.m.) the Treasurer of Gray's Inn (handsome and invigorating Leonard Caplan QC) meeting me in the snow to tell me that I had been elected an honorary Bencher of Gray's Inn. (I am the first, I believe, to be a Bencher of three Inns.) On getting to my room, a fine book awaiting me from The Solicitors of England and Wales signed by their admirable – and courteous – President, John Palmer. It was a faithful reprinting of the 1629 classic, John Parkinson's *Paradisi in Soli* in which he describes the garden of pleasant flowers, the kitchen garden and the orchard – just as we have now at home. In the evening, a reception at Butterworths to launch *The Discipline of Law* with the Lord Chancellor (Lord Elwyn-Jones) reading to all the motion of congratulation set down – without precedent – in the House of Commons by its most distinguished members*. The next day, after court, signing copies of the book for the long line of students waiting outside the bookshop beside the law courts. Followed a day or two later by acclamations at lunch at Gray's Inn and at dinner at the Middle Temple.

Soon afterwards a dinner in my honour by the Western Circuit – my own circuit – where I started and which I love – with the leader, Lord Rawlinson, proposing my

* Publishers' Note: The text of the motion reads: 'Salute to Lord Denning. That this House salutes Lord Denning, the Master of the Rolls, on his 80th birthday; expresses its warm appreciation of his long record of service to the nation as a judge; and records its gratitude for his outstanding contribution to the humane development of law and the administration of justice in Great Britain'.

health in the most felicitous of speeches. Followed a few days later by a dinner at Lincoln's Inn in the New Hall (new in 1845) full to overflowing – with the Treasurer, Sir David Renton, at his most eloquent: present also our Bencher Margaret Thatcher, soon to become Prime Minister – the 14th member of the Inn to be Prime Minister of England. Later by a luncheon in my honour by the Law Society of Hampshire at whose Quarter Sessions I had my first briefs and made my first mistakes.

In the Easter vacation a visit to that other London in Western Ontario where I was made an honorary Doctor of Laws. I told the truth to an academic audience: 'The trade unions are above the law'. Only to be received back in England with yells of abuse – and much comment. There was a General Election pending!

In the Whitsun vacation the televising of us at home – in my library and in the house where I was born – with David Dimbleby gently drawing me out. The best part was of my wife and me in our lovely garden by the Test. It was all too short.

In the summer vacation at the opening of the new Law Courts in Vancouver. The Courts, all of glass, cover many acres. I ventured to remind them of the old proverb going back to Chaucer: 'Those who live in glass houses should not throw stones'. Only to be assured that their glass house is unbreakable. It does not matter how many bricks are dropped in it or on it.

Then there was the production of a selection by me of literary pieces, performed by the Bar Theatrical Society at the Theatre Royal at Winchester: followed by a banquet in the Great Hall of the Castle. Sitting under the Round Table of the Knights, I recalled the words of Tennyson in the *Idylls of the King*. I knew them from my youth up. They were a spur to me then. He described the Knights as

'. . . . that fair Order of my Table Round,
A glorious company, the flower of men,
To serve as model for the mighty world,
. . . .

248

To ride abroad redressing human wrongs,
To speak no slander, no, nor listen to it'.

And so to live as to be inspired to

'Teach high thought, and amiable words
And courtliness, and the desire of fame,
And love of truth, and all that makes a man'.

I set those ideals before me in my young days, though I know that I have not been able to live up to them.

The finale for my birthday was a memorable evening at Lincoln's Inn. It was the most appropriate of settings. The Old Hall (built in 1540) was filled full to the doors and windows. We took from the first chapter of *Bleak House* the scene in that hall 150 years ago: 'At the very heart of the fog sits the Lord High Chancellor . . . *Jarndyce v Jarndyce* drones on'. On the wall of the hall beside us was Hogarth's famous painting of *Paul Before Felix*. So we took from the Acts of the Apostles the occasion when Paul was brought in bonds before the Roman Governor: 'Paul, thou art beside thyself: much learning doth make thee mad'. We described the crowds who threatened Lord Mansfield — his portrait is there in Lincoln's Inn — and his answer to them: 'We must not regard political consequences; how formidable soever they might be: if rebellion was the certain consequence, we are bound to say "fiat justitia, ruat caelum" '. Towards the end of our readings two of our young people sang that moving song of the First World War, *Roses in Picardy*. And I followed:

'Picardy — 1914 to 1918 —
Roses, Yes — and Poppies too.
'I was there. I saw them — in their thousands waving their heads — away back — behind the lines. But at the front, over the top of the trench, there was no-man's-land, scarred and bare.

'Out of us five brothers, three fought in Picardy. I was the youngest of the three — only there for the last nine months. Too young to go before. I came through unhurt. The other two were soldiers there from the beginning. Both were in the battle of the Somme in 1916. Reg, the second son, in the attack up the hill at Pozières — he fell severely wounded. Shot through the head, he lay on the ground — given up for dead — for 5½ hours — while the tide of battle rolled to and fro over him. At length his comrades found him and carried him back. He survived.

'A little later Jack, the eldest son, was killed leading his men into action at Geuedecourt. He was only 23. He wrote in his copy of Palgrave's *Golden Treasury* — on the flyleaf — in pencil — the words of Kipling's *If.* We will read it to you soon.

'I remember the telegram coming. Mother opened it with trembling fingers. "Deeply regret . . . died of wounds". She fainted to the floor.

'A few days later came a letter which was found in his valise after his death — to mother and father. He wrote:
"This may be my last letter to you, because we are for it, I think, tomorrow.
If I do get pipped, you may rest assured that I shall have done my duty".

'Mother and father — poor dears — they were to lose another son before that war was over. The third son was Gordon, the sailor. A midshipman in the Battle of Jutland. Just 19. In the destroyer *Morris* covering the battle cruisers. The first to engage the enemy fleet. In the despatches he was "commended for the cool and skilful way in which he, as officer of quarters, controlled the foremost 4″ gun, primary control having broken down". Soon afterwards he was stricken with illness due to his ordeal and died courageously. He is buried in our country churchyard. "Home is the sailor, home from sea".

'The fifth son, Norman, was also a sailor. Too young to serve in that first war. But in the second, he played his part. In an underground room of that concrete fort next the Admiralty, called the Citadel. Under the rain of bombs, throughout the war, his Naval Intelligence kept track of those enemy ships — more powerful than ours — day and night

without ceasing. *Bismarck, Tirpitz, Scharnhorst, Gneisenau.*
Till they were defeated. Winston Churchill joined them in
that room from time to time.

'Reg is now a General — retired. Norman is now an
Admiral — retired. But Jack and Gordon — they were the
best of us:
"They shall not grow old, as we that are left grow old:
Age shall not weary them, nor the years condemn.
At the going down of the sun and in the morning
We will remember them" '.

The poppies slipped from my hand to the floor. Eyes filled
with tears. It was the eve of Remembrance Day. At the end I
said to them:

'If you can fill the unforgiving minute
With sixty seconds' worth of distance run,
Yours is the Earth and everything that's in it,
And — which is more — you'll be a Man, my son!'.

251

Index

257